The War Zone

A Story of
Christopher Columbus Homes
Newark New Jersey Projects

War Stories

People Who Lived There

2nd Edition

By
George Langston Cook
B.S. History

ISBN
978-0-6152-4065-7

Barringer High School

Branch Brook Park

Sacred Heart
Cathedral

Clifton Avenue

Colonnade
Apartments
C & D Building

Mt. Prospect Avenue

Garside Street

New
McKinley
School

Old McKinley School

Cutler Street

St Lucy's

Wood
Street

Crane Street

Sixth Avenue

Sheffield
Street

Sheffield Drive

Christopher
Columbus
Homes

Stone Street

Summer
Avenue

Summer Place

Seventh Avenue

High Street

Colonnade
Apartments
A & B Buildings

Webster
Jr. High

Webster Street

Broadway

To Downtown

To North Newark

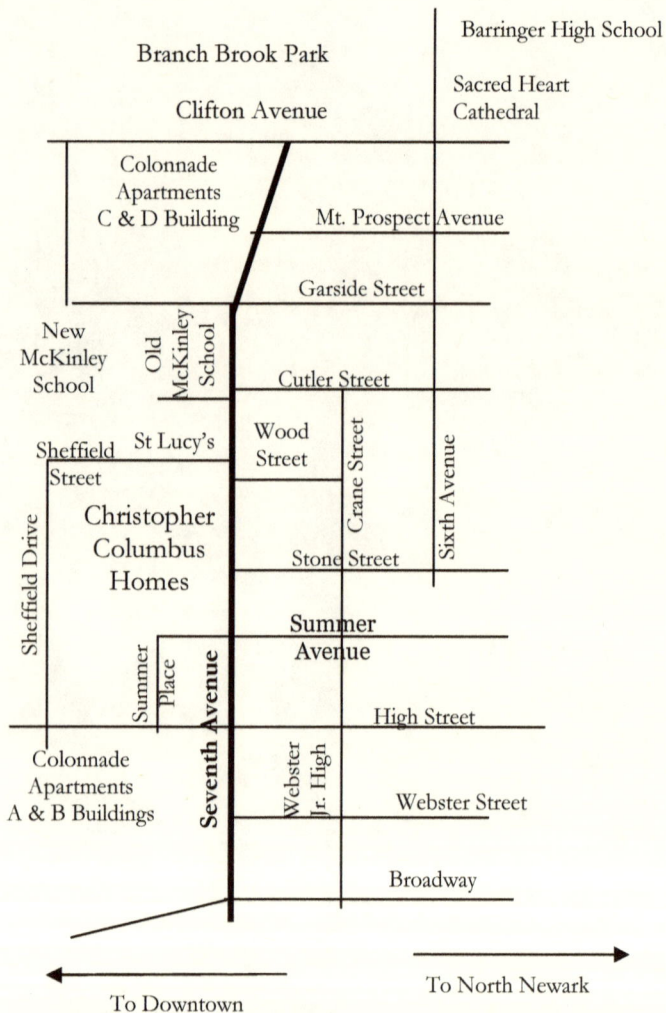

The Columbus Homes / 7th Avenue Neighborhood

4

If you can imagine 8 buildings constructed in a similar style to this only two stories taller, standing on one city block, with two large playgrounds, parking lots, and a community center then you can just about imagine Christopher Columbus Homes. (See the layout below) Pictured here is one of the Senior Citizens' buildings at Kretchmer Homes off Dayton Street in Newark.

Sheffield Street

14   16

Courtside

10   12

Playground

94   92

Courtside

84   82

Wood Street

Parking Lot

Playground

Parking Lot

Stone Street

74   72

Courtside

64   62

Seventh Avenue

6   8

Community Center and Office

Flag Pole

Summer Avenue

Courtside

2   4

Parking Lot

High Street

Smoke stack

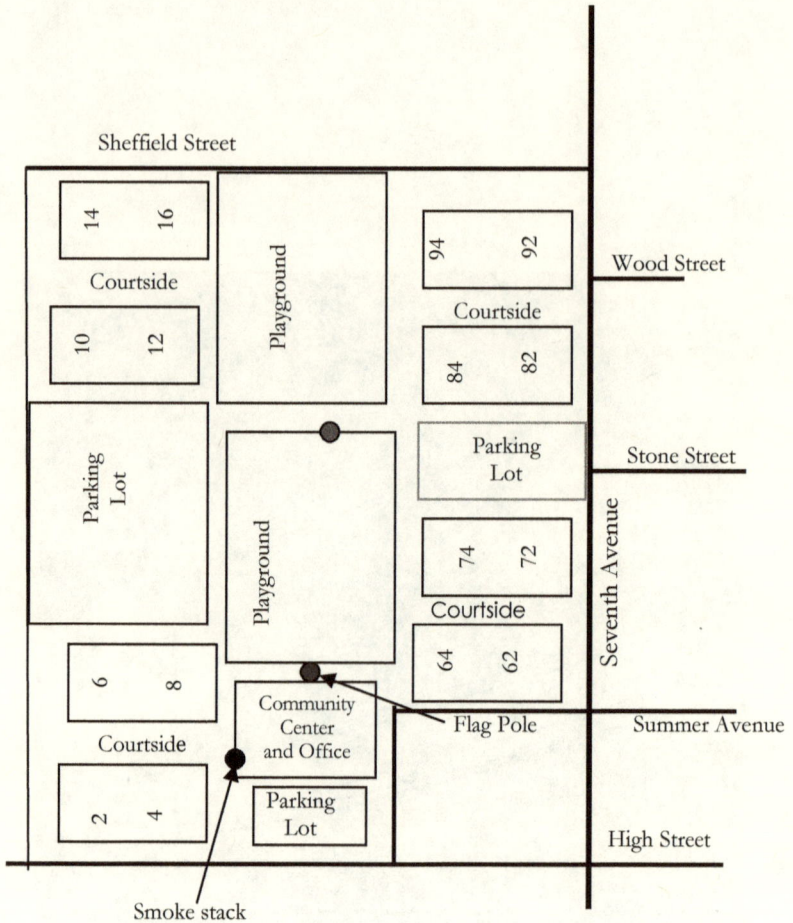

Christopher Columbus Homes,
Newark New Jersey Projects
Layout

6

Neighboring H
Apartment

Front Stairs

Public Hall Way
To B, C, D, E, F, G
apartments,
and back stairwell

Elevator
shafts

Girls' Room

Front Stairs

Boys'
Room

Foyer

Bathroom

Living Room

Parents'
Room

Kitchen

Neighboring B
Apartment

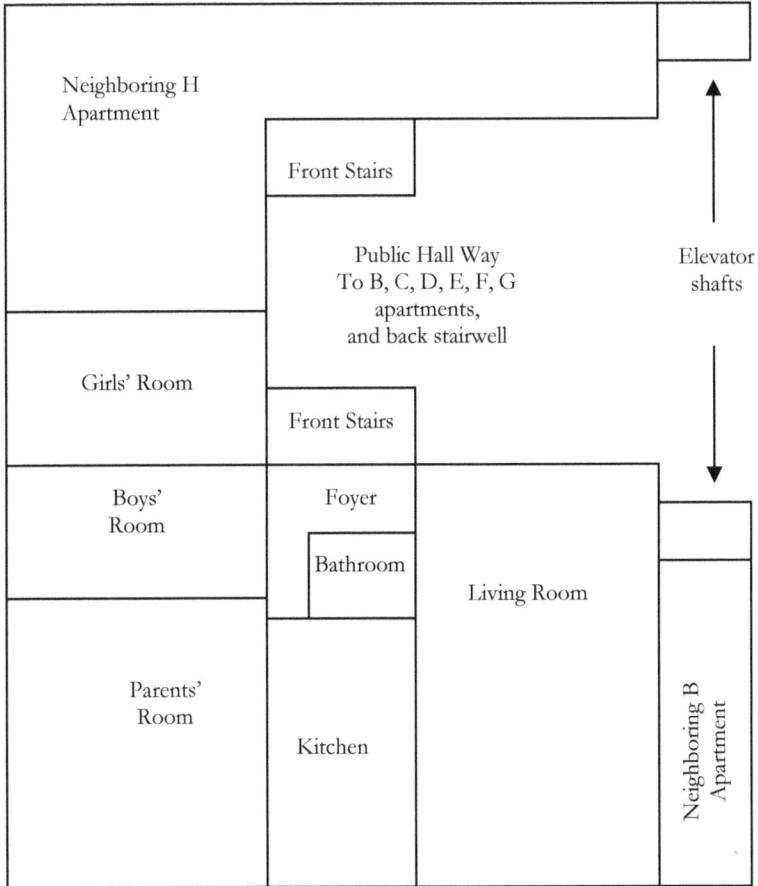

Columbus Homes
84 Seventh Avenue 1A Apartment Layout
1956-1982

Dedication

This story is respectfully dedicated to the memories of the Brothers and Sisters who didn't' make it, the families of the dead, injured, and the survivors. Spill a little wine off the top for them.

A special dedication also goes out to the city officials and housing authority policies of Newark, New Jersey, for without them this story and others like it could never take place. Let's pray they receive their just due.

Introduction

Whenever I go online to perform research, I often spend some time revisiting Newark, New Jersey the city where I grew up. I find negative accounts of living there overwhelming in comparison to the positives, especially those stories depicting life in the hi-rise public housing projects that have now been almost totally demolished. Even some former residents of many of these types of federal housing projects with whom I have discussed their views mouth the same negatives. Their description as hideous, non-viable, or poorly planned blights to surrounding neighborhoods that festered with crime and drugs belies another reality. I hope my story straightens out many of those misconceptions.

Were hi-rise apartment complexes inappropriate for family living? Many of the comments about those public housing projects suggest that people weren't meant to live on top of each other as they did in Columbus Homes and in similar settings. How does that statement, spoken as if fact, explain the increasing number of hi-rise condominiums being built in cities across America, or the multimillion dollar hi-rise apartment buildings on New York City's Fifth Avenue? Why is it that these developments aren't projected to fail as did the public housing projects? Why are not they described as incubators of crime and despair? Does the failure of these places fall on the shoulders of poor people who lived there or are other factors involved?

I grew up in one of these complexes, and my family spent thirty years living in it. That place was Christopher Columbus Homes, the Seventh Avenue Projects, so please consider my opinions as being biased, filled with conjecture and innuendo. Though I admit mistakes were made and bad influences came to inhabit them, I sincerely doubt that neither the places nor the inhabitants themselves were the cause of their problems. I remember Columbus fondly in some aspects and tragic in others. My belief about what transpired there centered not only on my understanding of the place, and the people, but the politics and management as well. Where do I begin telling my story of Christopher Columbus Homes, the Seventh Avenue Projects that once stood in the North Ward of Newark, New Jersey, and the

9

people I remember from growing up there? Why must these tales be told? Well, I believe they deserve to be told.

Where to begin is difficult to fathom. Recent happenings remain fresh to the mind; results of the past defy denial. The old neighborhood is now demolished. Once a place inhabited by talented artisans, athletes, and beauty queens changed to a slum boarding many hapless residents, left to live there among the infestation of rats, roaches, and drugs. It never was a ghetto for the word is too pretty to describe it. From its glorious beginnings it became a dirty slum, a crying shame and a war zone.

Why did hi-rise housing fail? Residents of Mt Prospect Towers, a private building at least partially funded with help from HUD, and the several similar hi-rise apartment buildings in Newark complain of loss of maintenance and security standards despite much higher rents. This building is now more than 25 years old and shows decay and decline.

I began recounting stories of the people, places, and events from my youth while teaching in Phoenix Arizona more than twenty years ago. The environment, characters, and incidents I mentioned intrigued my students since most these kids had no real concept of what living in a high rise apartment complex was like.

Phoenix at that time derived much of its character from its wide open spaces, vistas of the nearby mountain ranges, and relative isolation from any other major city. Single family homes were the norm in this large and now very populous city. Its urban/suburban sprawl spread out for tens of miles in all directions, and its living spaces seldom traveled skyward unless you consider that building on local peaks as being high rises. Even the poor live with space to maneuver in, as their neighborhoods rarely included structures taller than two stories, and single home lots measured 6000 square feet minimally. This resembles nothing like the Newark, New Jersey I knew in the fifties, sixties, and seventies.

In 1960, Newark ranked as the 30th most populous city in the United States with a population over 405,000 people. It also bore the distinction of being among the nation's most densely populated cities as well with more than 17,000 residents per square mile. Consider the entire population occupied less than the twenty-four or so square miles making up the city limits. At the time I started telling the stories of the people I grew up with to kids, Phoenix may have had a population of about 790,000 but encompassed an area of 324 square miles with a density of less than 2500 residents per square mile. In comparing 1980 Phoenix to the density of 1960 Newark, the U.S. Census Bureau did the math.

Most families lived in the multi-family buildings that outnumbered single family dwellings to squeeze all those people into the city. Newark's older three and four story tenements were built in the late 19th and early 20th century. They housed from six to twelve families each. Three or four of these tenement buildings could easily fit onto my small Phoenix home lot.

Additionally, the old tenements lacked modern electrical wiring, plumbing, and heating resulting in poorly lit cold water flats. Electrical, coal, and gas fires were common especially in winter. Their brick faced wood framed walk-up construction and cramped corridors made these tenements firetraps. A fire in one apartment easily destroyed the whole building and also damaged neighboring structures.

Some larger privately owned and managed buildings built in the early 20th century were constructed with better materials, brick and brownstone. They seldom rose above four stories, or had more than a few apartments on each floor. They bragged of larger rooms, higher ceilings, hard wood floors, and modern conveniences. Their oil heating was centralized and they had hot and cold running water. They were generally more exclusive than tenements which outnumbered these buildings by far.

Beginning during the Depression years, the new Newark Housing Authority started building "the Projects," a series of multi level public housing complexes, averaging three stories in height, in every section of Newark. The NHA also planned, built, and managed projects throughout the post WWII era, a time when Newark's total population actually shrank. The NHA built most of its high rises in the fifties and sixties.

These mostly red brick, hi-rise buildings housed more than 10,000 families into their confines. By contrast to the tenements, the projects were well lit inside and out, and were wired to meet the demands of the then modern appliances. Though the rooms were smaller and ceilings lower than the privately owned buildings, the layout of their grounds compared favorably, all having playground and court areas for the residents.

Their solid construction included metal fire doors as the entry point to each apartment. Each individual residence was also fireproof from the ones next door. They were also designed as fallout shelters during the "red scare" and cold war atmosphere to accommodate the masses. Rarely would earlier constructed privately owned apartment buildings meet that standard of protection for its residents. The Projects were truly built to last much longer than they actually did.

The names of Columbus, Walsh, Scudder, Hayes, Bradley, Kretchmer, and Stella Wright represented the tallest and most populous sites. Places named Baxter Terrace, Fuld Court, Stephen Crane Village, and Pennington Court had far less height and fewer families, yet the same atmosphere found in the high rises permeated these residences as well.

The several privately owned dwellings in Newark modeled their hi-rise apartment living partially on the Projects. Places like Academy & Garden Spires, the Ivy Hill Apartments, Abington Towers, Georgia King Village, Zion Towers, Mount Prospect Towers, and the Colonnade Apartments fall into that category. Today only where management and maintenance levels have diminished or management has decided to overwhelmingly accept Section 8 dollars as a means of sustaining their rental income have these compounds declined from their previous grandeur. Many of their residents receive public assistance and rent subsidies as well.

This picture of Academy Spires was taken from Branch Brook Park. Since they now take Section 8 dollars things are not as nice as this view shows. Not shown from this view is how people hang out in front and near this once exclusive complex.

Perhaps it was a flaw in their design that made the Newark Housing Authority responsible for utility costs of used by the residents. Even failure to pay rent never lead to the loss of those services, and many residents took them for granted. No home heating system I've ever encountered compared to the steam heat running through the Project radiators and piping system during the winter. Anyone who lived in the public housing projects rarely complained of the cold as was true with private housing. This construction flaw seems to have been mostly eliminated by privately owned high rise apartments.

I returned to Newark in 1985 and told the same stories as I substituted in the schools there as well. Those students were just as amazed as the students in Phoenix in the people and experiences I told them about. Obviously, the characters and their stories deserve the merit for the ability to hold the attention of people from as diverse backgrounds as Phoenix and Newark. I hope you too find this truth just as interesting.

March 7, 1994

Imagine this scene if you can, experiencing it as if you were awakening from a dream. They appear to stand there, majestic, proud, strong, towering over most of the nearby landscape like a series of reddish sandstone buttes rising up from a dark and desolate desert floor. Count them. The uninitiated eye captures eight, but the informed mind knows that sixteen exist. Yes, sixteen huge red brick apartment buildings, joined together in opposite facing pairs to give the appearance of eight single structures, constructed on a single city block. As the eye follows each from the ground skyward, thirteen stories stand out. But how can that be, for is not thirteen an unlucky number in construction?

Walk to the center of the grounds by the yellow fire hydrant, and face southward. Two twin pairs of these monstrous shapes split the sky. A large blacktop parking lot with three aisles each with opposite side horizontally angled parking spaces separates the two sets. A narrow shaded courtyard sits in the middle between each pair that is separated by that lot.

Beyond that southern view is a thin road that splits the compound off from the slightly elevated heavily traveled highway to New York City, just ten miles away. Beyond the highway, commuter railway line rushes people to a nearby station then on to Harrison, Hoboken, and New York. Finally, a splendid panoramic view of the downtown Newark skyline opens up to the southward facing eye.

Turn around 180 degrees towards the north. Two more pair of these edifices catches your eyes. Just as with those on the south side of the block, shaded courtyards rest between each set. The parking lot on the block's north side contains only a single double sided aisle whose measurements are much shorter than the large lot. Beyond those buildings lies "the Avenue."

Now look towards the east. There lies a large field that ends abruptly after some seventy yards at a ten-foot tall steel mesh fence. In the middle, between its north and south ends, the fence opens to an empty flag post in front of a short, oblong, two-story building. A huge phallic shaped smokestack rises as perhaps the tallest structure within this complex, and it stands as if a sentry at watch, silently overlooking the grounds from behind the one short building.

To the west is another playground, one that rivals the first in size, but is broken up by a basketball court and an enclosed kiddy park complete with benches, cast iron monkey bars, and round sandboxes.

Standing next to these soon to be demolished high rises is like being in a ghost town. Even the trees appear to be dead

Walk westward through this playing field to the street marking the compound's border with the outside world. Across this narrow street sits a much larger peculiarly shaped locked fenced in playground with a school occupying its far side. The narrow street between the complex and the schoolyard runs south, then races east, to become that thin road separating the projects and the highway. As it curves eastward, a footbridge crosses above the

15

highway and commuter rail line. Face north one last time and see past the schoolyard to a small Catholic church occupying a fenced lot accompanied by its Bingo Hall that makes contact with the Avenue.

Across the Avenue, the spirits of the past whispered on the wind. No stores, bars, or street life exists to remind them of the activities once prevalent here. Only rented two level town homes that replaced the decayed wooden and burnt out brownstone tenement buildings and remaining open lots witness what little traffic now flows along this once busy artery. Something here is very wrong. There is nobody here.

This neighborhood appears dark, even on this bright autumn morning. Leave the Avenue! Run back towards the buildings! Look around carefully! Not a single car occupies any parking lot. Tall weeds and uncut grass grow up through the concrete and asphalt. An occasional rat scurries along empty sidewalks, searching for food scraps tossed from the open windows of passing cars. Only ghosts inhabit this place, as it appears no living man, woman, or child has walked these paths in quite a while.

Stand next to one of the buildings, and the spooky sounds of the ghosts abound. The window frames are devoid of glass, and you hear the wind slamming wooden doors open and closed on the upper floors.

Hastily erected concrete barriers block the buildings' entrances in a poor attempt to discourage vandals. First and second floor window frames underwent the same treatment as the entrances. Imagine these obstacles work as a means to deter only the homeless and the helpless, for only they may attempt to find solace here. Rain furnishes the only running water, and lightning brings the only apparent electricity. Thieves have long ago stolen the metal doors, pipes and plumbing fixtures. No one can live here!

Wait! Something is in here. There are wires, running everywhere. Why? Walk around the grounds again for a closer look. Those two large fields can't be playgrounds. They're covered with asphalt. That basketball court, why it's lopsided and filled with pot

16

holes large enough to lose a car. That kiddy park is, oh my God, made of concrete, the benches are all broken, and the sandboxes... why... they're empty! Beer cans, broken glass, and... what's this... hypodermic needles and crack vials strewn about everywhere! What a mess! Wait! Wires are out here too.

Now the buildings bare their wounds to the eye. Graffiti spray painted on many of the outer wall. What does it say? "W.I.C.K.E.D.S." What does it mean? Was it some kind of gang that once lived around these stone structures or perhaps a curse placed upon long gone inhabitants? What happened here? What does any of this mean? Can anyone hear? Is anyone listening? No one answers.

Signs appear. Names... directions... all covered with spray paint. Scratch off some of this mess. What does it say? Yellow ones with black writing and symbols posted above what once were entrances reads, "Fallout Shel..." before the strain gets to the eyes and causes a slight headache. A sign on the short building says "Office," while at another entrance a different sign reads "Community Center." No one is inside, and the yellow colored walls are covered with something black... soot... but there is no sign of fire damage. Puzzling! Maybe that smokestack contributed.

One more sign with engraving. The spray paint can't hide its message. "Christopher Columbus Homes, 112 Eighth Avenue, erected...

Wait. Why does the name ring a bell? Something you read in the Star Ledger this morning. What did it say? Oh yes... a federal housing project, Columbus Homes, built during the housing shortage during the 1950's is set to be demolished this morning at 9:00 am...

Wait again. This is no dream!

Demolished! 9:00 am! Quick, check the time. It was 8:30 when I arrived here, and it's 8:58 now. RUN! Where? Towards the Avenue, climb the fence surrounding this site. Faster... don't stop. Run up the Avenue to Cutler Street and run towards its

17

intersection with Crane Street. 8:59... other people stand there, waiting... Listen... Hear the warning siren... heartbeat's racing... almost out of breath... Remember. Remember growing up here? No more people here! No more life! No more time!

For a moment nothing happened then a flash of light momentarily blinded the spectators followed by what seemed like the force of a jackhammer tearing through concrete. A thunderous roar filled the air, carrying with it a brief rustling breeze. An eerie silence then overcame the gathering throng.

The buildings shook like an alcoholic needing a drink then swayed like drunken men ready to pass out. The high roofs sagged in at their center, while what can be best described as their spines evaporated. The roofs continued falling straight down, taking floor after floor with them on their journey, until those buildings, those once towering, majestic, and proud red-bricked structures crumbled into several piles of sky high rubble. A cloud of fine dust debris rose up and floated towards on-lookers as if to blind them from the final degradation suffered by these magnificent buildings.

Several sky high piles of bricks and rubble was all that was left.

Initially, a raucous cheer and shouts that an eyesore is gone came from the assembled masses. New development and growth can now take over where the weeds once inhabited. Their faces seemed familiar. They witnessed all of the City's high rise demolitions. Reporters from local tabloids interviewed them. City

18

officials present smiled and shook hands. Yeah, they're happy, but they never lived here, never really understood.

Other familiar faces congregated away from the city officials and around the town kind of folk. I huddled together with them, hugging, sometimes laughing, as we reminisced. We told the stories of our families, and asked the "where are they now questions" of old friends and associates. Sometimes the answers actually disturbed whoever asked.

My eyes didn't see clearly anymore, as some kind of wetness covered them. Umm! Tears! I didn't know that watching this would have such an effect on me. But then was not the time to cry. A solemn pledge needed fulfillment.

I left the crowd and walked slowly towards the ruins of that second building from the Bingo Hall along the Avenue, avoiding guards placed there for "my safety". I sneaked through a hole in the fence and moved quickly towards where the west playground met the second pile of rubble. I bent down and took one before scurrying like a rat through the fence again.

They owe me this... this one brick... and I am taking it. One of the legendary stories of this Project is that my family lived here so long we probably placed last brick in Columbus, so I'm taking it back.

One brick for all my brothers and sisters, my mother and my father, for every year this place provided our home, for every tragedy suffered... for everything. Damn right they owe me this, and likely much much more. But one brick will do to satisfy the Cook Family legend. I'll bring it back when the war is over.

The Place

The memories of a four-year old boy generally lack specific details, but I remember Columbus Homes from back then very well. My family moved into the projects one week after my fourth birthday. It smelled and looked like a new place then, being completed earlier in the year.

We occupied a first floor corner apartment that no one had ever lived in before. Pastel colors filled the walls of the five and a half rooms. The waxed and buffed dark colored floor tiles glistened with alternating patterns. Every window that could open had screens. Heating radiators shined from fresh coats of aluminum paint. Paint camouflaged the pipes leading to upper floor radiators with the same color as the room they were in.

A heavy gray metal front door to the apartment opened into the living room or the front room as we called it. A wooden door for the narrow linen closet attached on the left side wall as you entered the front door. The room's oblong shape stretched from the door to the centrally positioned window some eighteen away. The door less kitchen was placed toward the room's right side close to that window. The view from out the four pane wide window looked east and down on the south end of a narrow parking lot, where cars parked horizontally to its sides. Building 74 was located directly across the parking lot some eighty feet from my window.

The small, eat in kitchen came supplied with a gas stove and refrigerator, both new. The kitchen sink perched between the stove and entrance on the west wall, directly opposite the window. Open wooden shelves hung above the refrigerator's cubby hole on the south wall. The kitchen window's view also faced east, and contained about a ten by ten foot fenced in landscaped area with a newly planted young tree. The parking lot and 74 also filled that visual scene, along with the north to south view of the large asphalt covered east ball field, and the office building. A concrete sidewalk stretched around the field.

Back towards through front room opposite the closet door, another wooden door opened to a narrow foyer leading to a bathroom and other wooden doors for the three bedrooms. A long closet space with a double shelf above and a post for hanging clothes hid behind the hallway door. Beyond that, an open closet space across from the bathroom door filled the length of the hallway. A ceiling light guarded the entrances to the three bedrooms at the far end of the twelve-foot foyer.

The bathroom contained the three most needed plumbing fixtures, and a small medicine cabinet above the sink.

The right side bedroom shared a wall with apartment 1-H. It contained a recessed closet space and a single window. Looking immediately down, a small chain link fenced in lawn with new trees planted near each side ran the width of the building. Just past it is the concrete sidewalk, the large west playground, and the buildings and parking lot of Sheffield Drive are seen through this south-facing window. Looking through that parking lot contained the downtown skyline's panoramic view. This became the girls' room

The middle bedroom was the smallest of the three. It had no closet, but had the same southern view as the right side room. This became the boys' room.

The corner windows in the left side bedroom made it unique. One side of the windows faced east, the connecting side faced south, as the room was situated on the southeast corner of the building. Two cubby-holes serving as closets also equipped this room. This became my parents' room.

A pastel yellow colored brick faced hallway stretched to the right about ninety feet after leaving the apartment and connected the seven other apartments on this floor. Starting from my apartment and down the hall and around to the one opposite our door, they were labeled alphabetically from A to H, along with the floor number. Our apartment was labeled 1-A.

Apartment 1-H facing my apartment door is the only other three-bedroom apartment on the floor, the other six having only two. Its living room window faces west, onto the narrow shaded courtyard between it and Building 94. Wooden benches surround the raised flower boxes seen through the living room and kitchen. A narrow roof extends from just under the living room window, covering a porch entrance to the building. All the shaded courtyard buildings' entrances had this structure.

Back out in the hallway, two metal fire doors, each positioned just outside the large apartments' doorways lead to the two front stairwells. Well lit and maintained, the gray painted concrete stairs with steel banisters on each side and yellow glossy wall bricks lead up to the twelfth floor and down to the lobby. One stairwell side runs up even further, to the roof. There were thirteen steps between each landing; except for between the first floor and the lobby there were sixteen. Posted on the wall of each landing and each floor's hallway a sign read "No Loitering-Under Penalty of Law".

Down the hallway the other six apartments' doors rested across from each other in three pairs. Between my apartment and the one next to it is the odd elevator door, named so because it only opens on the odd numbered floors, the lobby, and the twelfth floor. A hatch for the garbage chute was situated between the second and third apartments on my side of the hall.

Another doorway at the far end of this hallway led to the backstairs. Its stairwell led up from the back entrance to the building to the twelfth floor. There a ladder rose to a hatch for the entry onto the roof. A fire hose long enough to reach each apartment on the floor was folded and hung on each landing next to the connection to the fire main. All twelfth stories were laid out in this fashion, the only difference being the two elevator doors placed on opposite each other in the lobby and on the twelfth floor.

The front stairwells emptied into the lobby. Between their doors and the exits, the green metal elevators doors faced each other. Next, mailboxes for each apartment were enmeshed into opposite facing walls. Beyond the mailboxes are sets of four pairs of one way swinging doors, two pair for each exit, the courtside or parking lot side. Going out by the courtside exit three other doors come into play before getting out the building. Two are for the use of the janitors, the third being the lobby apartment. These lobby apartments had as many as five bedrooms, and I think even more.

Exiting the building to the parking lot side found a room directly below my apartment and the one next to us that peopled used for storage. Once outside you see the incinerator room, which is where the garbage chute emptied.

A wide sun exposed patio ran north towards Seventh Avenue between the building and the parking lot. Building number 82 attached to my building just past the back stairwell entrance. It was a good fifty-sixty yards from the storage room of my building to that of building 82. A long inclined concrete ramp coursed its way from near its storage room door down to the sidewalk of Seventh Avenue.

Most all of the buildings were laid out in this fashion, except for the four buildings having a single front stairwell instead of two, or two lobby apartments instead of one. Maybe the outside architecture varied somewhat, but not tremendously so. Also each window's view depended on the building and the floor and room it was located.

Every other building had a laundry in their lobbies. Each building was surrounded on three sides with a ten foot wide swatch of landscaping. Concrete framed wooden benches added emphasis to the complex, around the east playground, and on the courtsides of each building.

The project's boundaries included Seventh Avenue on the north. Summer Avenue and High Street bordered it on the east. Sheffield Drive curved from High Street to Seventh Avenue to cover the south and west end of the complex.

Seventh Avenue stretched nine relatively short blocks from Broadway up a thirty degree rise to Clifton Avenue. Though the whole distance could be walked in about ten minutes, it supported every type of commerce the community needed. Columbus Homes' residents frequented the business establishments on Seventh Avenue.

Quite possibly, every service a person needed from birth to death was found there. Hardware stores, vegetable stands, dry goods, grocers, doctors, dentists, bakers, barbers, butcher, fish market, luncheonettes, liquor store, all small family owned establishments, on the ground floor of tenements. Most kept the charm and atmosphere of the Italian neighborhood, dominated by St. Lucy's Roman Catholic Church, which preceded the building of Columbus Homes.

If you traveled straight north from the parking lot in front of my building you'd find yourself on the intersection of Stone Street and Seventh Avenue. Nappi's Luncheonette on that northeast corner stood as the morning stop for police officers from all over the city and the entire maintenance staff at Columbus. The thought of their sausage sandwiches with potatoes, peppers and onions, and the eggplant parmesan still makes my mouth water.

Walking east between Nappi's and Summer Avenue were the dry cleaning store, the 7th Avenue Pharmacy, A&C liquors, a small factory, and a gas station. Across Summer Avenue from the gas station Gabriel's, a tavern, served freshly baked pizza that is still the best I ever had stateside. Then there was Mayers, the "supermarket" of the day that would be swamped by just one aisle of today's grocery stores. Many young boys from the projects made tips carrying orders from there to customers' nearby apartments.

Following Seventh Avenue to High Street there was Arres' Bakery right on the corner. Their Italian breads and rolls, pastries and cakes left nothing to be desired. I acquired my love for apple turnovers from visiting the store. Those who experienced it know what I'm talking about.

Regardless of how good the Arres' products, Giordano's bakery, only a few doors down on the next block heading towards Webster Street, never lost business to them. The only other store I remember on that block was a walk-down Chinese laundry that prepared shirts starched and ironed for a very reasonable fee. The only other structure on the entire square block was Webster Junior High, or as we called it Big Bad Webster.

Between Webster Street and Broadway I only remember the tenement buildings and the Star Auto Supply store on the corner of Broadway. Across Broadway the Seven Ciccolini Brothers furniture store stood out. Broadway itself heading north the two blocks to Bloomfield Avenue had many more stores including a Woolworth's and Seibels. From the corner of Seventh Avenue and Broadway a leisurely walk southward to the middle of downtown took no more than maybe twenty minutes.

Heading west on Seventh Avenue again, across Stone Street from Nappi's was Carmine's grocery with its short tight aisles. The owners there at first seemed mean to me (maybe because when I was five they told my father that it was me who stole and ice cream sandwich from their front freezer. They were right.), but they also stayed the course in the neighborhood until they were burned out in 1974. They also opened an ice cream store right next door.

Between Carmine's and Wood Street, a hardware store, a fruit stand, a small bar, a few stores I don't remember, then the Old Mill Tavern on the corner of Wood Street. The Brookdale Soda Company was located on Wood Street along with a number of tenement buildings.

The other corner of Wood Street and Seventh Avenue had my favorite Italian family grocer. D&D's (which we often called Tip-Tops) made coming in the store a treat. First they were friendly, funny, and often did tricks with coins to make a kid laugh. They also hand made their brand of own spaghetti and grated cheese.

Right next door to them was Celantano's. This store appeared to be the most modern with florescent lighting and wide aisles. The sold sliced meats and cheese like most of the other grocery stores, and made take out sandwiches on Italian bread and kaiser rolls. Of course their prices were higher too. There was also a dentist office on the second floor of the next building.

Pop's candy store was on the first floor of a walk-up tenement. The old guy running the store was an easy mark for snatch and runs for the penny candies and cookies he kept on the front counter. Almost every boy hit him up at least once as if it were a rite of passage.

Lucy's fruit stand came next. Fresh fruits and vegetables were always available there. She, her husband and son lived in my building on the fifth floor. The next store was one of the dry goods stores, before it became Po' Boys, famous for their potato sandwiches, submarine sandwiches, and Italian hot dogs. There was a Cuban bakery, and once a bridal shop that followed Po' Boys and the fish market on the corner of Cutler Street. Right around the corner of Cutler Street, sat Mario's candy store, and the live poultry store.

The United States Savings Bank stood on the west corner of Seventh Avenue and Cutler Street. Though moved to a different location, and taken over by a larger institution, it still operates in a small mall on the corner of Seventh Avenue and Mt Prospect Avenue. Next to the bank, Fede's may have had the best sausage sandwiches in the world, served on quarter cut round Italian bread, with onions and peppers, and topped off with mustard or ketchup. Hmmm good!

Moving towards Garside Street there were a few more tenements and repetitions store types from previous blocks. A store we called the post office guarded the northeast corner. Another Italian bakery sat few doors in on Garside Street.

The oldest section of McKinley Elementary School stood across Seventh Avenue. At that time a new building was still in the planning stage for the lot across the street from Columbus Homes. The school's second oldest section was separated from the old brownstone main building, and ran along what became Colonnade Place. It contained the gym, cafeteria, and grades four through six. The old school building, after several changes in name and student serviced was demolished, leaving a playground for St. Lucy's Elementary School.

Seventh Avenue crosses Garside Street and Mount Prospect Avenue to the corner of Clifton Avenue where it terminates at

Rotunda Pool. Across the street from the pool was the south end of Branch Brook Park.

A clear view of the New York City skyline was easily seen from the top of Seventh Avenue. From the top floors of some Columbus Homes buildings, the Statue of Liberty and Palisades Amusement Park stood out.

Two large dirt covered lots, one on the south side of Seventh Avenue between Garside Street and Clifton Avenue, the other between High Street and Broadway became the Pavilion and Colonnade Luxury Apartments and the new McKinley School building.

St Lucy's Church dominated the block across Seventh Avenue from Po' Boys. In addition to the church, the complex included the rectory, a bowling alley, the site for the Bingo hall; St Lucy's School, an order of nuns, and the National Shrine for St. Gerard, the patron saint of Italy. Father Ruggierio who delivered his homily in Italian was pastor of the church, and two young priests, Father Granato, and Father Nativo performed mass as well.

Each October, the Feast of St. Gerard ran three to four days and drew crowds from across the nation. All the streets intersecting Seventh Avenue would be decked out in lights and heavily populated with carnival rides and vendors stands selling foods, toys, clothing, and Italian memorabilia. On the Saturday and Sunday of the feast, the St Gerard Statue was marched around Italian North Newark, and people pinned dollar bills as it passed.

The smell of Italian sausage cooking with onions and peppers filled the air along Sheffield Drive in front of the church. Though it was an Italian festival, the people from the projects enjoyed the food and activities regardless of their race and nationality.

In the earliest days living in Columbus Homes, the milkman delivered his products, as did the bread man. The insurance man stopped at the house weekly to collect his premiums. Even doctors made house calls there. One street peddler in particular would sing out every time he traveled up and down Seventh Avenue. I never knew what he sold, but I can still mouth out the sounds he sang loudly to attract customers.

A year round recreational program operated at Columbus Homes. Organized activities were held in the Community Center/Office building. Mr. Fiore, Mr. Gianella, and Mr. Federicci checked out balls and umpired games played in the playgrounds during the summer. Arts and crafts available held after school to the kids, taught many of us how to make lanyards for key chains from colorful flexible plastic strands and other activities. I believe the first plastic models of planes and ships I put together were supplied through the Columbus recreational program. Ballet and tap dancing classes were also given in the Community Center, along with the first few years of Mr. Wilson's karate classes.

On hot sunny summer afternoons, Mr. Fiore, Mr. Gianella, Mr. Federici, or Mr. Russomano opened the fire hydrant between the two playgrounds, and attached a showerhead to it. So many of us would dress in swimsuits, take towels and blankets outside, and spread them out at our favorite spot on the Sheffield Drive side of the east playground. We'd run in our bare feet underneath the watery spray to stay cool then we would lay down on our spaces. Sometimes we'd throw water on our easiest targets, or drag someone into the water's mist.

Scouting was also available initially to the boys and girls At Columbus. Different residents served as scout masters and den mothers over the years. This continued as an activity up through the early 70's.

McKinley Elementary School that served Columbus Homes and from Seventh Avenue to Crane Street addresses also provided after school recreational activities. We spent many hours in the gym built with the new building, and the downstairs recreation room. Since the Columbus Homes outdoor basketball courts got in the way of the softball games, many of us polished our games at the McKinley hoops.

During the winter months, fifth and sixth grade teams of Rocha-Russ, Bellat-Agresti, Major-Ciccone competed at indoor kickball

28

games. During the spring, the games came outside, with punch ball for the boys and kickball for the girls.

No discussion of this neighborhood could be complete without discussion of how it was kept. The grounds and the buildings were well maintained. Trash receptacles were placed at every building entrance and other strategic points around the complex. Janitors swept and mopped down every floor and stairwell daily. The incinerators burned the garbage on site and the janitors emptied them three times daily. Twice a week the city sent garbage trucks to cart away the burnt debris. Burned out lights on every floor and landing were replaced on a daily basis as well. The outside grounds were either swept or raked, paper picked up and properly disposed. The maintenance staff often times would give twenty-five to fifty cents for the young boys that helped with those daily chores.

Columbus Homes also possessed two street sweeping machines that were used to sweep down the sidewalks and playgrounds. The last thing anyone had to worry about was the cleanliness of the entire facility.

Additionally, the maintenance staff included glaziers, painters, inspectors, and elevator repairmen. In the event of a broken window it was replaced within a day. If the elevator "got stuck" someone came immediately to remove the unlucky passengers. If an elevator broke down, it took no more than a few hours to get it working again.

The apartments themselves were inspected every six months for damage, and the eviction for property damage was a real threat. In addition they were repainted every two years automatically, or whenever someone moved out.

Logistical considerations made where Columbus Homes was built important. It was a short twenty-minute walk to downtown. It was even closer to the main branch of the public library and the Newark Museum. Columbus Homes and vicinity served as the catchment area for McKinley Elementary School, a Webster Junior High School, plus Barringer and Central High Schools, which were all reachable within a few minutes on foot.

Seventh Avenue was within a few blocks of McCarter Highway, a state road that ran north to Passaic County and south to the Newark Airport, while connecting to three major US highways. Two of the four bridges crossing the Passaic River to Harrison and Kearney did so within a quarter mile from Columbus Homes.

Columbus Homes was serviced by a few bus lines that ran down Seventh Avenue from Bloomfield Avenue, and down Summer Avenue. That does not include those serving the major arteries of Clifton Avenue and Broadway-Broad Street. Also the Newark/Broad Street station for the Lackawanna Commuter rail line with a connection to New York City was within a stones throw from Sheffield Drive.

When you also consider the proximity of Branch Brook Park and Rotunda Pool, the Columbus Homes Project seemed to lack nothing. Schools, recreation, culture, local commerce, transportation services and infrastructure, and management combined to make the living a pleasurable experience as seen through my eyes and those of many others.

The second section of the old McKinley School building is still being used. The section that was on 7th Avenue was demolished in the 80's for a St. Lucy's school playground.

30

The People

There were one thousand five hundred fifty two apartments squeezed into Columbus Homes. That meant a lot of families lived there as well. Some people you never forget. The same is true for the families at this one housing complex, on this lot.

Many individual and families inhabit my memories and it would be unfair to miss any but it's impossible to include them all. I'm sure to receive some feedback from those not included. For that I apologize now.

Italians initially made up the single largest group of residents, followed by Blacks, then Puerto Ricans. I remember names of white families like Martino, Beasley, Baker, Barlow, Winquist, Gladys, and West from my building. I formed bonds with the Wynn, Howard, Jackson, Hunter, Epps, Coleman, Harris, Hines, Evans, Saunders, and Fisher among the black families there. God, just writing this makes me think also of the Herbin, Dickinson, Flowers, Pendergrass, Archie, and Cauthen families as living in my building at one time or another.

It would be thoughtless for me not to mentions some of the legendary family names that lived in throughout Columbus Homes. Starting on Sheffield Drive there were the Jenkins, Jones, Reynolds, Howard, Rivera, Vasquez, Echols, Beale, Fortune, Walker, Laurel, Hughes, Lowery, Willoughby, McGhee, Hinton, Harding, King, Hawkins, Cabel, Rivera Bowman, McDaniels, Palumbo, Conger, Darby, Watson, Green, Workfield, Wilcher, Hurtt, Melvin, Smith, Kidd, Wheeler, Mann, Buglione, Davis, Coleman, and Woodson just to name a few. Then in the 7th Avenue buildings there were Cook, Wynn, Miller, Scott, Jones, Garland, Brown, Butler, Martinez, Correa, Cunningham, Walker, Clark, King, McCray, Hicks, Lobianco, David, Aikens, Thomas, Edwards, Andrews, Raines, Turner, Stevenson, Rogers, Hayman, Daily, Spiers, Bracey, Irving, Bailey, Cobb, Caporella, Peterson, Petrocelli, Plant, Price, Roach, Santiago, Sawyer, Scott, Sheilland, Stewart, Twitty, Johnson, Vining, and many more than I can truly remember at this moment. Remember, there were 1552 apartments at Columbus Homes!

31

Even though Columbus Homes was public housing, initially few poor or welfare dependent families lived there. It was first a working class neighborhood, dominated by the traditional nuclear family structure of two parents with children. Senior citizens also lived in these projects right along with the young and large families in the beginning.

It would be difficult to speak about Columbus without first mentioning the family of my best friends, the Wynns. Mr. Jordan and Mrs. Mary Wynn initially lived in building 74 on I believe the 11th floor, but then moved into my building just down the hall to 1-E. There was no apartment I was in more than theirs as the eldest son Jordan and I were months apart in age, he less than a year older than my brother Michael, and Jimmy their middle son was within two years of me. The youngest Wynn, Kevin, and my younger brother Glenn were the same age too. Greater than with most other families from Columbus, the Cook and Wynn families are still very close more than fifty years later.

Seated are cousins Al Edwards and Jimmy Wynn; Standing are Jeffrey Edwards and Jordan Wynn. The Edwards lived in Building 82, the Wynns on my floor in Building 84

Ms. Ginny, Virginia Howard and her family lived on the twelfth floor. It was the second most favorite place to visit because she

32

always welcomed the whole gang of us in her home. I think she always saw all us boys as if we were her sons. Her having all very lovely daughters until I was nearly out of high school helped too.

Picture of Virginia Howard courtesy of Sussie Howard

When we first moved in to the building a Mrs. Martin lived across the hall, but she didn't stay there long. Some kind of accident killed her infant child when she to fell off the roof to the courtside entrance porch underneath her living room window child. A Puerto Rican family moved in that apartment next, the Guadelupes. My sister always babysat for Esther during the eight to ten years she lived next door, and remained good friends until long after they moved away. Then the Kearney's moved in and after them came another family of Howards.

The West family lived in the lobby apartment of my building for several years. They were a large tribe. I mostly remember two of the youngest sons, Pete and Bobby, who were much older than me. What made them stand out so much in my mind was the softball games held in the east playground.

Bobby and Pete starred in the fast pitched contests played in the evenings and nights of summer. From my parents bedroom window we had a perfect view of the diamond, though sometimes we chose to lie on the steel mesh fence overhanging home base.

Mr. and Mrs. Baker, a middle aged couple lived on the second floor, and their window overlooked the building exit on the parking lot side. I remember how they yelled at us using that bare spot of wall to play three flights up. We kids thought they were just too mean, and so they earned the nickname "the landlords."

Mrs. Epps and her four daughters lived directly above us, and she filled the spot of my mother's best friend until her death I think in '78. After her husband split from the situation and my father did the same in the second half of the sixties, my mother and Ms. Julia would have their Saturday night pint of gin and beer. Sometimes the result of their drinking wasn't pretty.

The joke about Ms. Julia was that she always knew what was going on, that she could hear through sound-proof walls and see around corners and through buildings. Funny, I missed her after she passed.

There were two little old white widowed sister who lived in apartment 10-B, Ms. Winquist and Ms. Gladys. Ms. Gladys hampered by severe arthritis never left the apartment and needed a walker to get around in it. Feisty old girl she was, always arguing with her sister about one thing or another in her gravelly voice. She reminisced about her youth when her now shortly cropped gray hair was once long and auburn in color. She was sure to show a clip of her hair she kept in a photo album, and to remind her sister it was auburn and not red. Ms. Winquist fussed more than argued with her sister. Widowed years earlier, Winquist made the household spending decisions. As the neighborhood worsened she relied on my sister or me to shop for them. I also would do their windows for them.

Some of the grown men in the neighborhood were hell-raisers, and you always heard them on Saturday nights. Nobody messed with a small cadre of them. Mr. Wynn, Mr. Bracey, Mr. Daily, Mr.

Stewart, and Mr. Sawyer were counted among the bold, loud, and irreverent, and there were others too. Mr. Wilson was the resident black belt (now he's an eleventh degree legend). Mr. Walker ran the Essex County Youth House, so none of us messed around while he was around.

I remember the Martino family from my floor fondly. When my brothers, sisters, and I were baptized at St. Lucy's, they stood up for us, becoming our god-parents. Their daughter Marie, one of my sisters' better friends caused her parents no end of heartache when she fell in love with Johnny Lugo, a Puerto Rican that lived on the 7th floor. I think they moved to prevent her from seeing him, which was good, because he ended up being a thug.

That was part of the atmosphere, tension between the three major groups, Italians, Puerto Ricans, and Blacks. But it's funny that everyone seemed to have associates and some good friends from each group. And it never showed up on the field during the spring to fall season softball games held in the large east playground.

The whole neighborhood seemed to ring around the fenced field during the games. Players represented each ethnic group and almost every building in the complex. Now I was too young to remember if the games were all intramural games, but I remember sometimes guys came in from other neighborhoods to play. The boys from Columbus Homes rarely if ever lost at anything.

Many friendly rivalries existed between the children living in different buildings, and between Sheffield Drive and Seventh Avenue sides of the complex. Though fights occurred, fists dominated as the weapon of choice, and a handshake as the inevitable conclusion. Most fights also ended with opponents becoming closer as friends.

A large number of exceptional athletes lived in Columbus throughout its existence. John Hawkins who lived on the Sheffield Drive side excelled in high school in three sports. Of course there was Bobby and Pete West, "Foots" and Gordon Jenkins, Ron and Warner King, Sam Clark, and so many others.

I remember one day we were playing football in the grass outside the Scott's building 74 lobby apartment's window. Henry, one of the older brothers jumped up to catch what he thought was a pass, and instead snagged a wren, one of those small fast birds in mid flight.

I remember Logan Wilkerson who lived in building 82 and what he brought to the basketball court. No taller than 5'10", he played often with his back to the basket using finger rolls and ball spinning trick shots to confound his opponents.

My own age group had a large number of exceptional athletes too. Keith Coleman was perhaps the best basketball player and distance runner produced by the Projects. At 6'2" he played the guard and forward positions on our high school team, and also jumped center. He averaged 27 points a game in our strike shortened senior year. Even as a sophomore Keith was also one of New Jersey's premier cross county athletes.

Irving Chapman may have been one of the smoothest ball handlers and all around basketball players. Bernard Brooks armed with accurate shooting, strong ball handling, and aggressive jumping made him more than just formidable. Albert Workfield, Harvey Workfield, Tommy Jenkins, Jay Foster, Tony Johnson, Harry Kidd, and the list went on for the basketball legends from these bricks.

I doubt if anyone would question that the Jones' from building 10 had a lock on football fame. From Jesse down through Chester, Joshua, and Jerome, they all played and excelled. Jesse even coached one of the city's high school teams.

Norman Beale lettered in football, track, and basketball, and was perhaps one of the city's best all around athletes. Jimmy Smith who did not play organized sports brought a singular aggressive quality to the athletic games we played. James and Allen Walker were perhaps the fastest swimmers I saw as a youth.

It's far more difficult to say who ran the fastest in the projects. Mikey Scott, Richie McCray, Clarence "Poochie" King, Carey Jackson all possessed blazing speed, but I'd put my money of Carl

36

"Skippy" Workfield. I once saw him give a sizable head start to James Bracey then beat him to the end of the field. Then some would say my youngest brother may have held that distinction, but then again, I never really raced him.

Then there were always fights or some kind of competition going on there. There always seemed to be a friendly natural conflict between the 7th Avenue and Sheffield Drive sides. Some rough house football, basketball, races, and many other contests took place the rest of the year. I remember how one group of us would chase another group of us, out of having fun or escaping fear. The competition was antagonistic many times, cooperative at other times.

I remember the fighters, especially the ones around my age, because I lost battles to many of them. Around the first day I moved in Columbus I got into a fight with Keith Saunders. Eddie Wilcher and his brothers could be rough on a guy. Petey Reynolds, Eddie Davis Jr., and Lonnie Coleman could be a bit of a terror too. Charles "Rock" Rogers, James "Scooner" and Melvin "Boobie" Bracey, and Gregory "Muffy" McCray always gave me trouble. Then there those who were so tough I just didn't mess with them too much. Larry and Jerome Jones, Larry Reeves, and Gerald Stewart are amongst them.

Some people from the neighboring blocks were considered familiars and were welcomed in Columbus most of the time. Among the most accepted were Pat Davis, Girod Simmons, Gerald Morgan, Joe Greer, Walter Porter, Dickie Smith, Larry Hight, and Stoney Carr. Some outsiders had to fight in order to pass by before earning the right to hang. Who of us can forget the famous Davis-Yancey brawls? Snowball fights in the winter often included the students at St Lucy's School because only a steel mesh fence separated their school playground from the one at McKinley.

If the Seventh Avenue and Sheffield Drive worked together at anything, it was to dispose of people from other projects. Though I never saw one, the stories of the fights on the bridge between Columbus Homes and Baxter Terrace, a much smaller complex on the other side of the rail yard, would make you proud. Baxter

Terrace, always considered to be in the Central Ward, always seemed to ally with Columbus Homes in those gang fights.

Columbus also had its share of musical talent. In the old days, groups would gather near 82's porch and croon do-wop tunes. Rumor has it that one of the guys, George Clinton, is really famous now, but he doesn't sing do-wop anymore. The Four Seasons also would drop in at Po' Boys and harmonize for a few. Local talent shows always brought out the star power of many of the residents. Beverly McLauren and Susie Howard sang like birds as did Norman Beale and Sherwood Hayman. The Echols formed a band that came out with an album or two. Then there was St. Lucy's Drum and Bugle Corps.

Newark throughout the late fifties and sixties bred some of the best drum and bugle corps in the country, and St. Lucy's sponsored one among the very best of them. On late spring and summer Saturday and Sunday mornings, they'd march up Seventh Avenue to Branch Brook Park to practice their routines. Other local corps would meet there too, as they took turns exercising cadences and licks.

I remember a day that appeared to have a cloudy overcast until St. Lucy's horns started blowing. I swear, the clouds parted and the sun came shining through. And whoever heard their rendition of the "Battle Hymn of the Republic" would agree it was without peer, and helped them win a national championship.

Besides that of the drum and bugle corps, music continued to play an important part of life in Columbus. I remember summer afternoons when some Puerto Ricans and Blacks would sit at the benches on the Sheffield Drive side of the big field, creating rhythms with various drums, and whatever could be used as percussion instruments. On warm summer nights along the avenue going back as far as the late fifties, individuals and groups would croon those doo-wop songs of the day. It is said that George Clinton, later famous for his Parliament and Funkadelic groups sang on the Avenue in this fashion.

The Echols family that lived in the lobby of Building 16 formed a band named "The Family Circle" and cut a few albums. There

38

were others that sang those sweet harmonies as well. Susie Howard and Beverly McLaurin did some singing together in the late sixties. And who can forget the singing performance at Barringer's talent show put on by Norman Beale and some other young men. The Willis Brothers continued that sweet vocal harmony tradition through the 70's and 80's.

In the 70's a few courtside porches welcomed those of us with audio equipment and music collections to contribute to the atmosphere. We played music from jazz to popular rhythm & blues through most summer days and evenings.

During the weeks before Christmas colored lights would of various patterns and designs began to dot the complex. By Christmas Eve many windows flashed with these displays, as Columbus Homes' residents provided an outward appearance keeping with the spirit of the season. The light usually sparkled in the windows until just after New Years Day.

Of course there were some quacks living amongst us as well. I also remember that more than a few troubled individuals used the easy access to the roof to leap to their end. A cross dressing gay Italian male from building 82 made his mark beating up his multitude of boyfriends, and being called from the window by his mother. If we mimicked her call to him, "hey Junior" he'd give us a halfhearted chase. Half hearted because he was one of the fastest guys in the neighborhood. He was openly gay years before "the Wall" brought many of his kind out of the closet.

Mr. Clark was an enigma of sorts. No doubt he was strict on his sons, and sent his sole daughter off reportedly to study in the Soviet Union. He kept the refrigerator door in his apartment locked. Also there was no doubt he was above average in intelligence and politically astute. He ran for governor in the sixties and garnered more than several thousand votes for a third place finish, amazing for a black man especially for one living in the projects of Newark during those times.

Joe and Vinnie Price used to get into their parents' money stash. Here we'd be near building 74 by the parking lot, and dollar bills would come floating down from their seventh floor window. They did not live in Columbus too long.

I often times found myself in the company of Mr. Raines who lived in building 62. Besides the fact he had daughters near my age, and that he lived across the hall from on of my best friends, what most intrigued me about him was his pet, a squirrel. The day I enlisted in the Navy in Norfolk, Virginia, I bumped into Mr. Raines' son Elliot as he was disembarking off the carrier, USS John F. Kennedy. Talk about it being a small world.

I remember when I delivered the morning newspaper I always had a problem slipping it under a particular third floor apartment door in building 64. Mr. Lobianco had plush sky blue wall to wall carpeting throughout the house. Perhaps he wasn't a quack, but that was definitely unusual for the setting.

Foots and his brother Gordon were good for a laugh anytime they walked by. They possessed natural comedic talent, and had the plethora of comedy clubs that exists today been around then, they would be famous, no doubt. Now, I looked up at them as the 'big boys' when I was only four to six years old.

Dennis Aikens who lived in building 62 and I often spoke about the old ladies who lived upstairs from him. We called them the "ladies in black", and attributed spooky characteristics to them. I think we both know now they were not really witches.

Now there were a whole lot of us at about the same age living between the buildings 84, 82, 74, and 72 Seventh Avenue. As young boys, aged three to six, we were already quite socialized, at least most of us were. My brother Michael and I, Jordan and Jimmy Wynn, David Scott, Joe Price and his brother Vincent, Bruce and Billy Wilson, Ralph Daily, Walter Brown, James and Allan Walker, Dwayne and Darrell Hines, and a few others always hung out together and competed against each other. Our parents socialized together as well.

At those early ages we picked our own leaders, and followed them in a game I wasn't very good at. Too clumsy I guess to follow the

40

fellows through the obstacle course laid out by the leaders. David Scott, though one of the youngest was usually picked as the leader.

We would usually have to go through the large concrete barrel between buildings 82 and 92, jump the swinging chains that served as the fence for the well kept hedges and large flower boxes, and climb the steel mesh fence that surrounded the large asphalt playgrounds. These were the easy things. All of us could follow.

David was amazingly nimble and dexterous for a four-year old. So when he would lead, instead of going through the barrel, we had to climb on top of the four-foot diameter obstacle. Instead of climbing the fences, we had to walk along its top support posts as if we were high wire artists testing the mastery of our balance. I definitely lacked proficiency at following these acts. In fact, I'd always end up at the back of the line, being one of those not very good at following the leader, even in those days.

Follow the leader wasn't the only game we played in those days. All of them tested our physicality. Some were ball games, like playing catch, three flies up, box-ball, or we shot marbles for "beauties", and spun our spinning tops. We boys played catch with small rubber air filled balls. Star pimple balls became the favorite over the regular pimple ball. We'd try to see who could throw the ball the highest against the building, or catch it with one hand after bouncing it off the barrel. Even some of those games challenged me.

We ran a lot of races too. We'd challenged each other, running from 84's incinerator room door to 82's storage room door and back, sometimes in relays. We'd race up to Sheffield Drive or from the Community Center around one or both playgrounds. We even outran the elevator and each other up to the twelfth floor and back down again.

Hopscotch, jump rope, and kickball contests also took up some of our time, along with the neighborhood girls. During the summer, when many of the parents sat outside in the late evenings, we'd play these massive games of hide and seek, catch one catch all, red rover, and we included the girls who wanted to play.

41

Exploring was another of our favorite things we boys liked to do. Mounds of dirt in the lots that became the Colonnades and the new McKinley School buildings provided hours of fun throwing dirt bombs in our war games. I remember playing Hula Hoop games, or making scooters from wooden milk crates, metal roller skates and a bed slat. If somebody had a red wagon, we'd take turns riding it 'down the hill', from Sheffield Drive to the Seventh Avenue side of the playground.

Some of us wandered up to the roof in our games. Warm summer nights up there gave us a wonderful view of the rides of Palisades Park which was about 10 miles away to the northeast.

As we got older others joined while some left our group. Robert Butler moved in when we were in the second grade along with his cousin Ricky Miller and nephew Mickey Scott. Hubert and Herbert Norris twins from building 64 often joined us. Joe and Vinnie Price moved away. We also began to include Keith Coleman and Jimmy Smith from Sheffield Drive, mostly because we were in the same grade and stayed out of trouble.

We followed the street down to Broadway where we'd find large discarded cardboard furniture boxes in front of the Ciccolini Brothers' store. We found a grassy hill we called "the Circle" that was formed by an exit from State Highway 52 W onto McCarter Highway S near the Passaic River. To get there we had to traverse through "Bums Alley," where a number of what we called bums often found themselves. We took the boxes and slid down the grassy hill and wrestled for hours at a time. Talk about having fun!

However hectic our day, we usually found the time to meet at our clubhouse, the back stairwell of building 74 between the second and third floor. There we'd discuss the hot button issues of the day, like who was the best super hero or baseball player. We'd theorize about dinosaurs or the sun the moon and the stars. We'd hike on each other until we found something else to do.

Of course, we boys were not angels all the time either, especially as we entered adolescence. I remember our play in the elevator. We'd enter on the lobby, push all the buttons, and run out.

42

Sometimes as a bunch of us entered the elevator we'd turn off the light and then start punching each other as it rose to the top floor.

There were some among us that were not always good guys. Some of the kids were more aggressive in many aspects than others. They'd use intimidation, pick fights, or play hooky from school. Though it's true none of us were saints, it was relatively easy to tell what a kid would get into by which group they belonged. Few guys were capable of being in both of the dominant groups however some people in our group were not intimidated by anyone.

I guess all of America was more innocent in those days before the assassination of President Kennedy. I walked from Columbus Homes to Watson Avenue in the South ward or to Peabody Place in the North ward, alone, when I was eight years old. These were trips of maybe two to three miles through heavily populated sections of Newark, without being attacked, chased, manhandled by strangers, or accosted in any way.

There were so many of us, we never felt the fears that strikes kids and their parents today. We initiated our own games and freely moved from one activity to another without the coaxing or coaching of grown-ups. We roamed throughout the complex, neighborhood, and city without worrying whether there was a "molester" hiding in the bushes.

Many of the parents either socialized together or at least everyone knew everyone. That made it easy for all grown ups to watch out for us kids, and report if we were up to doing wrong. Some parents even gave permission for other grown ups to instill discipline in children not their own. Getting away with being bad just seemed impossible… in the beginning at least.

Picture courtesy of Donald Jones

47

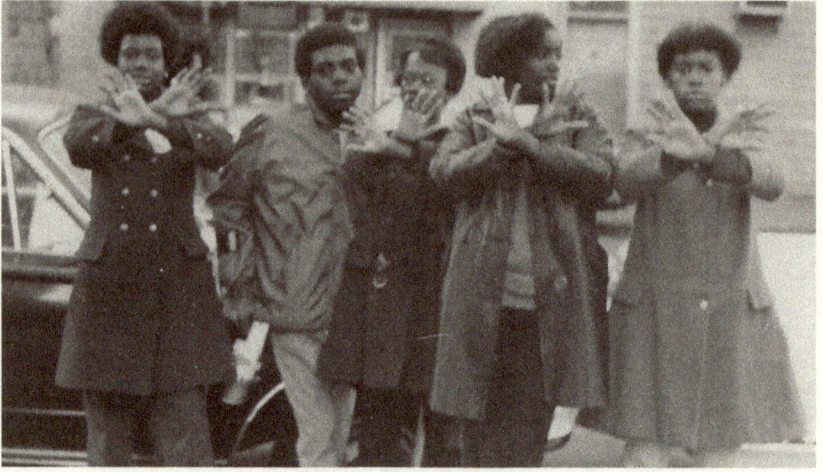

Picture courtesy of Donald Jones

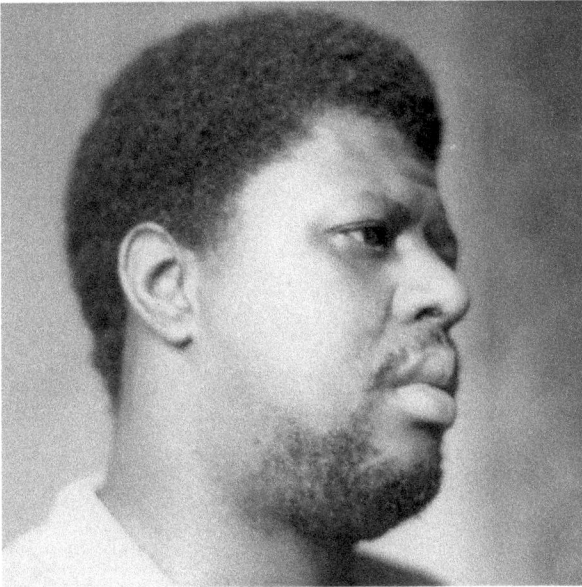

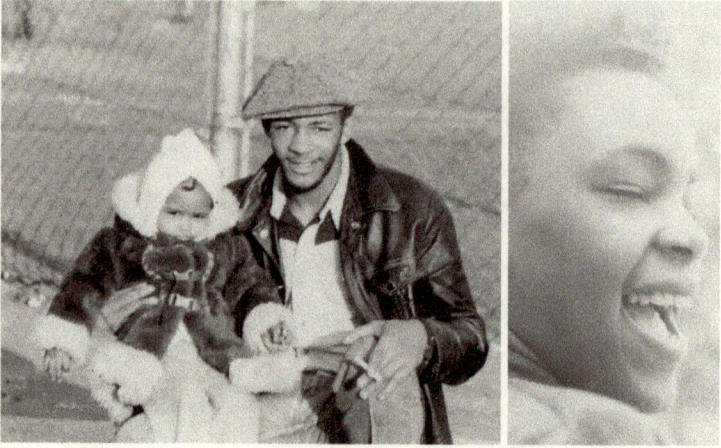

Picture courtesy of Sussie Howard

Thinking back to how it was makes me wonder why it all had to change. Surely if the status quo continued, I'm sure Columbus Homes would still be a vibrant community today. But over time revisions in the management attitude and maintenance schedules, plus changes in city building codes reduced the quality of life there. Increased numbers of welfare dependent families changed the atmosphere. The fall-out caused from the perception of the "riots" in 1967, 1968, and 1974 contributed to the flight of businesses from the vicinity. Working class families left to live in areas where services and supports could be found.

Columbus Homes and vicinity changed tremendously throughout the late sixties and seventies. The accounts accusing the NHA of poor planning, structure, and management fail to consider the initial make-up of this community succeeded, though it did change over time for the worse. Mismanagement, drugs, crime, racial fears, misappropriation of funds, and politics all contributed in some way to the destruction of this community.

The steady breakdown of washing machines installed in many lobby washrooms caused perhaps the first removal of services at Columbus. It was evident that the machines were not designed for the use of so many families. Lack of regular maintenance on those laundry room machines caused problems, too. In a few short years, this internal service was eliminated. Frank's laundry first on Crane Street, then on Seventh Avenue became the place where most people washed their clothes.

Beginning in the late 50's and early 1960's, the apartment inspections diminished in number and frequency, and fewer evictions resulted. Broken windows took longer to fix, and burned out hallway lights took longer to replace. Elevator repairmen, once a part of the Columbus maintenance staff, became scattered throughout the NHA. A week or longer would pass before a temporary elevator repair was completed.

In the summer of 1967 all the outside garbage receptacles just up and disappeared, not only in Columbus, but all over heavily Black populated sections of Newark.   Littering in the neighborhood increased. Paper wrappers, cans, and other trash generated outside apartments ended up on the ground.   Broken glass became common on the sidewalks and playgrounds. Cigarette butts were found everywhere.

During the seventies the maintenance staff decreased and its cleaning frequency changed. The maintenance staff once included one janitor per building that is two for every dual construct. By 1970 one janitor covered two buildings, and often failed to complete the work that needed to get done daily. The street sweeper machines that had at one time kept the playgrounds cleaned vanished, so it was rare if the maintenance staff swept more than the immediate vicinity of building entrances.

In addition, in 1972, perhaps due to new air pollution standards, the incinerators for burning trash were scrapped and replaced with trash compactors. It has been suggested that an associate of then Mayor Ken Gibson received the contract to produce and install the compactors.   These machines put in every building were not designed for the volume of garbage generated by residents. They broke down often and the garbage chutes on each floor remained clogged with trash. The unburned refuse drew rats, mice, and other vermin to it.

Some residents set the trash afire just to prevent rodents from crawling up through the compactor and out onto the floors of jammed open chutes. It got so bad the maintenance staff could not keep up with the spillage or the repairmen with the compactor fires.

The housing authority sealed the chutes on each floor by 1975, making it necessary for each resident to bring their garbage downstairs to dumpsters sitting in front of the old incinerator rooms. When elevators failed to work, which occurred quite often, bags of garbage could be found in the stairwells, or was tossed from upper floor windows. The maintenance staff soon became overwhelmed by the sheer amount of trash found where it never use to be.

In the light of decreasing maintenance standards, the tenants' association formed. It successfully organized and managed a years long rent strike, which ended in a court settlement in its favor. Rents became reduced.

By 1982, the NHA reduced the number of occupied units in Columbus Homes from 1552 units down to less than 450. First around 1978, it closed the four buildings along the section of Sheffield Street renamed Ruggierio Plaza. In 1982 all the buildings on Seventh Avenue, including perhaps the best kept buildings in the complex followed suit. It moved the residents it could into Sheffield Drive units or other projects throughout the city. It also culled itself of those residents behind in the rent.

The management tried addressing the garbage and trash issue using measures that failed to increase maintenance staff. They paid 'floor captains' a small monthly stipend to sweep their hallway floor, and bring the trash downstairs. In many building and floors, the residents refused to cooperate with that remedy. The trash and compound cleanliness remained issues until the remaining buildings were finally closed.

Instead of a thriving community that added to the coffers of local businesses, by the late 1980's the NHA had evacuated the complex and bricked up all the buildings' entrances. It scattered the remaining residents to newer poorly built town house developments or the older three story court apartment complexes.

For several years Columbus Homes laid unoccupied, used only by homeless ex residents in between incarcerations and drug dealers. One scene of a Harrison Ford movie was filmed there. After a series of court cases, the NHA demolished them in explosively dramatic fashion. A new town house style development put in its place by early 2000.

Additionally, the City Council passed building codes greatly reducing new housing units allowed per acre. The building of high rise apartments all but stopped in the less affluent neighborhoods as the City committed to townhouse construction to solve its housing problems. That commitment may also have contributed to the diminishment of care and concern of the Projects, despite the apparent success of many privately held high rises along the Mount Prospect and Elizabeth Avenue corridors.

Also, in 1960 the Colonnade/Pavilion luxury apartments were completed at the top and bottom of Seventh Avenue. This added more than eleven hundred apartments in the area between Broadway and Clifton Avenue. The Colonnades were built to serve white collar business professionals and their families, a different class altogether from the typical blue collar family in Columbus Homes. They also demanded different level of service than the old community could offer.

Changes in the business establishments serving Columbus Homes occurred and affected the feeling of community. The building and occupation of the Colonnade Apartments also strained the Seventh Avenue business infrastructure. Mayers', the supermarket of the day made renovations to the store thus making it true competition to the mom and pop Italian grocery stores. The Food-Town grocery chain brought out Mayers before 1966. In 1962 between Garside Street and Mount Prospect Avenue, another larger supermarket opened, Food Fair. It was built to better service the food shopping needs of the Colonnade's residents. Food-Fair was a true supermarket by the standards of the day. Multiple aisles, expanded frozen food sections, and modern shelving style made it possible for shoppers to pick their own items and not wait in line to be served.

Between Food-Town and Food Fair, they offered much lower prices and a greater variety of products than the smaller stores could offer, but they lacked the inter-personal interactions that dominated the older Seventh Avenue establishments. This contributed to a changed atmosphere on Seventh Avenue itself.

There is no doubt in my mind that the drug use scourge brought many problems suffered by Columbus Homes and vicinity. Along with the heroin epidemic came the crime to support its habits and the trafficking. Older women shopping on the avenue or on Broadway fell victim to drug related crime as heroin addicts snatch pocketbooks. An atmosphere of fear hung over the neighborhood because of those assaults.

I can only guess at by whom and why that this menace first arrived in the neighborhood, but I can remember hearing in the third grade drugs were no good as early as 1960. I can also remember being approached in the sixth grade by an Italian classmate who lived on Cutler Street about getting some dope. I declined and never saw him much more until 30 years later when I was employed as a drug rehabilitation counselor.

Drug use became endemic of the neighborhood. Where during the sixties heroin was the problem that directly effected relatively few people, by the late seventies and early eighties crack cocaine trafficking destroyed what little civility was left in Columbus. Those families left there felt trapped or stayed because of the drug availability.

Many young men and women caught up in the heroin addiction resorted to snatching pocketbooks, burglarizing homes, or robbery to get heroin money. Some went as far as to pull stick-ups at the nearby commuter train station, or rob bus drivers. For the first time it was not safe to be alone in Columbus' halls, as muggings became common place.

The crimes perpetrated by heroin addicts, made it necessary to move mailboxes once mounted in each lobby's walls near the elevators into locked mailrooms. Eventually a resident handled all mail services out the Community Center.

The NHA response to this crime wave was to commit an increased police presence to Columbus. This by itself led to increased arrests of young black boys, for drug use or other related offenses. Of them, many got caught up in a life of crime they could never escape, while others escaped. No dent was made in the drug trafficking. It actually increased in the police presence, and some people say with their assistance.

During the mid to late seventies, trafficking out of Columbus increased due to the presence of major competing factions. It started small with marijuana, and heroin mostly sold from a few individual apartments. After a while a system developed that co-opted whole floors and eventually whole buildings. Rarely would the Newark Police Department send officers into those buildings. It took federal interventions, which succeeded in only temporarily slowing down the trafficking in Columbus Homes in the middle eighties.

Before returning to Newark in 1985 from Phoenix, I spoke to a Caucasian, Jewish, Vietnam Veteran who was receiving treatment for depression. He was very curious as to where in Newark I would be living. When I mentioned Columbus Homes, he perked up and began espousing the wonderful dope there. When I asked, he said he had never been there but knew from his sources that a very high quality of heroin was sold there. Upon arriving Newark, I relayed the story to several authorities. They agreed with the vet's assessment.

It is obvious to me high quality heroin did not grow up through the sidewalk of Columbus Homes. And those crime networks had to get their products from somewhere. And if the greatly reduced number of residents there in 1985 relied mostly on welfare income, how could those meager dollars support a drug operation with runners, look-outs, security, guns and bullets twenty four hours a day, seven days a week, year in and year out? You do the math.

The early to mid sixties marked a period great change demographically in Newark. Many Whites began moving to the suburbs of West Orange, South Orange and Livingston, as the Black population grew, especially in the Central ward. In addition, many landlords of the old tenements reaped a small fortune by provided little or no repairs in the already substandard housing, despite collecting rents and other monies. Fires in these buildings became common, and the landlords collected the insurance, but rebuilt nothing. They ran out on Newark, and their residents, mostly poor, mostly Black ended up in the projects. These trends continued through the mid to late seventies.

The fires were never really a problem in Columbus Homes but the surrounding vicinity suffered decimation by them. The first buildings destroyed stood along Wood Street and its intersection with Crane Street. A few buildings on Cutler Street and Garside fell next. The buildings on Seventh Avenue to go were across the street from St. Lucy's Rectory and the old McKinley School building. And after 1974 when actual businesses burned down, the only ones to rebuild were A&C Liquors, Ida's grocery which was established there only in the late sixties, and the 7th Avenue Pharmacy. Many of the blocks to the north of the projects appeared as if a bomb hit them, and remained like that until St. Lucy's became the first to redevelop them with new housing.

People often speak of the 1967 and 1968 riots in Newark as what contributed to white flight and black plight, however there is enough empirical evidence indicating the trends began before those days of civil unrest. What I remember about the 1967 riot was that Blacks stormed the 4th police precinct following a white police beating of a black cab driver. This occurred near the corner of Seventeenth Avenue and Belmont Avenue, in the middle of that part of Newark most densely populated and nearly 100% black. This was a good two miles from Columbus Homes that could still boast of more of an ethnic balance. Despite the fact no rioting occurred in our neighborhood, within two days from the beginning of the central ward unrest, armed State Troopers and National Guardsmen patrolled through Columbus and harassed many of us.

One day, while they were walking through the playgrounds, they started yelling then shot at several buildings, blowing out tens of windows. Had not the buildings been constructed with the materials they were, several innocent people would have died. Several days later, after the guardsmen and troopers were recalled, large numbers of Italian families began moving out.

I recently read an account by a former resident who wrote of the same incident, and said he believed they were shooting at snipers on the roof. I would want my old friend to know the only presence on the roofs of Columbus during the "riot" was a police presence.

What transpired after the 1968 turbulence seemed even more destructive to the old Columbus fabric than the 1967 riot. In that year fires destroyed hundreds of older city tenement buildings and the wood framed apartment buildings in the Central Ward. On the days following the assassination of Martin Luther King, a fire set on a single night burned blocks of these tinderboxes. The police arrested a thirteen year old black boy for the arson, but never explained who gave him the large sum of money they found on him.

The people who had lived in those tenements were thrust into various projects, including Columbus Homes. The careful screening that once kept some influences out was dropped in the wake of this housing disaster. It was with this throng of people moving in that Columbus began losing its working class neighborhood standing, become more of a haven for welfare dependent families. Once the delicate balance with welfare and working families was lost, nothing got it back again, like Humpty Dumpty.

Just prior to a 1974 city wide election, Columbus Homes became rezoned as part of the Central Ward, though it had been part of the North Ward. By this time Columbus was predominantly Black and Democratic. Rumor has it the rezoning took place as an effort to secure the North Ward council seat for Anthony Carino, an Italian from the "old North Ward" political establishment who was receiving pressure from other opponents. Mr. Carino kept the seat until he retired in 2002. I can't say for sure what the motivating factors may have been for the rezoning, but I can speak to how it affected election outcomes I have seen.

Also rarely spoken about was the Puerto Rican riot that occurred in the summer of 1974. It had the most disastrous effect on Columbus Homes and vicinity. While enjoying Puerto Rican Day celebrations in Branch Brook Park, a young girl became entangled and trampled by a horse rode by a police officer. Enraged by the event, crowds of Puerto Ricans left the park and marched down to City Hall. At City Hall the marchers were turned around and they angrily headed back towards the North Ward where they lived predominantly. Once they arrived at the corner of Seventh Avenue and High Street renamed to Martin Luther King Boulevard, they began smashing the windows and burning just about every Italian owned and operated store. Food-Town and Food-Fair stores were either destroyed by the fires or robbed by looters.

Most of the Italian owners never rebuilt their stores, sold the businesses, and left Seventh Avenue and other areas destroyed that one Sunday evening. The loss of those establishments changed the complexion of Seventh Avenue and the North Ward forever. Puerto Rican owned bodegas became the dominant grocer in those areas from that point on. Even today no large supermarket operates north and west of Broadway and Seventh Avenue within Newark.

Part of those negative changes resulted from the atmosphere of corruption that permeated throughout the NHA and other city agencies. Scandal followed both elected and appointed city officials.

Older Newarkers can remember that the mayor from 1962-1970, Joseph Addonizio, was convicted of a series of offenses that landed him behind bars for several years in the late sixties. The federal and state authorities have also investigated both mayors, Kenneth Gibson (1970-1986) and Sharpe James (1986-2006), with many of their aides and appointees ending up in jail. Some councilpersons were also caught in scandalous affairs.

There is little doubt that the NHA was party to some below board activities and political infighting as well. In the wake of what became known as Newark's race riots, the federal government provided the Newark and the NHA with tens of millions of dollars to alleviate some tensions within the City and the projects. Monies allocated for repairs at Columbus meant to shore up leaking roofs into twelfth floor apartments ended up being used to place security lights on the roof tops. As a result, every twelfth floor and access to the roofs was blocked off, residents were moved to lower floors.

An attempt to construct a kiddy park in the west playground ended badly. Whoever the NHA contracted for that task succeeded in painting part of the asphalt playground green, and embedding a few monkey bars. Some contractors built concrete sandboxes, but brought no sand to fill them. In the years after whoever took that money and ran, I never saw little children play there. To make matters worse, they raised a lopsided basketball court on the west playground that deteriorated due to potholes.

By the late 1970's, the NHA bought into the myth that the high rise experiment was a failure, and stopped all attempts to repair them. It became policy to raze the buildings until lawsuits and HUD, which supplied the NHA with large sums of money, stopped them until they met other conditions. That is why Columbus Homes sat empty for years since before 1988 to eventually being blown up in 1994.

Many past Black residents attribute pressure from St. Lucy's Church to the eventual destruction of Columbus Homes, saying race was their primary motivation. Being Black and a former member of that Catholic parish, I understand the sentiment but I also disagree with it.

To the credit of my antagonists on this matter, their argument is appealing. The neighborhood surrounding Columbus Homes was no longer a white neighborhood. It had been Italian, going back to the late 19th Century. It's also true many Italians from that neighborhood chafed at the destruction of their proud First Ward tenements when Columbus Homes was built. Anthony Imperiale who lived on Summer Avenue fanned the flames of racial tension between Blacks and Italians in the late 60's and 70's with his 'brown shirts." Additionally the rezoning of Columbus Homes into the Central Ward in the 70's to secure Anthony Carino's North Ward council seat smacks of racial overtones between Italians and Blacks, who had become the numerically dominant ethnic group in Newark and in Columbus Homes.

St. Lucy's did benefit from the housing stock loss in the neighborhood because it bought the land and built replacement housing it now owns and manages through another corporation. It also was able to acquire part of the Columbus Homes lot to build a roman style plaza in front of the church. However, the idea the church wanted to rid the neighborhood of non-Catholic Blacks belies the reality that many Blacks occupy their Villa Victoria housing units.

The Good News

I am currently a teacher in Phoenix, Arizona. One day a student at my school came running into my classroom. Out of breath from running, she announced to the class these words. "Mr. Cook, my grand ma knows you from the hood." I had to tell the young lady it was not really possible because I was not raised in the South Phoenix neighborhood where the girl lived. She then said, "No, not this hood, the real hood, back East in New Jersey." It turns out her grandmother was Flora Cooper, sister of Rose Gray, a long time Columbus Homes resident. Ms. Cooper has since that time told me some very interesting stories of my father, whom she was very close to in age. Imagine being 2500 miles from Columbus Homes and running into a family from there. It seems being a small world understates the coincidence.

Many individuals and families left Columbus Homes. Many families grew out of project life, buying homes in other parts of the city and other municipalities. Some of the young men and women who went to the military just never came back to the projects. Some went on to college life and allowed their education to lead them to a more prosperous lifestyle. Some kept contact with the neighborhood, some did not.

I had a chance to visit in Newark during the Christmas season of 2007. I spent time with my family and had a chance to see a few of my old friends. I came back again in the late spring of 2008, this time with the purpose of updating the contents of my book's first edition. Word got around and before long I was receiving phone calls from Columbus Homes' residents from the "good old days", some I had not seen or heard from for over 30 years.

I found that many people I saw during my visit have prospered in a lot of ways. Some of my friends' parents are still alive, while many of my old friends are now grandparents. When we spoke about the days we spent in Columbus Homes, agreement and disagreement shared in the conversation. Some expressed their own opinions as to what happened there and why. All in all, my visit sparked good hearted debate and spurred many memories.

Many of my own memories of the people I knew and knew of received a couple of good kick starts too. I was re-introduced to Mr. and Mrs. Eddie Davis Sr., the parents of associates long gone. I ran into friends not seen or heard from in years. I even found an old friend living in a nursing home. My only regret from the visit was my loss of contact with many of the old Caucasian and Puerto Rican families that once lived in Columbus Homes.

I heard St. Lucy's had sponsored a Columbus Homes reunion late in the summer of last year. It turned out that the actual sponsors belonged to a few of the old guard Columbus Homes families; the Walkers of building 64, the McRaes of building 92, and the Hicks of building 62. Many people I spoke to did not hear about it until too late and did not attend, however, some did. The event did not have wide publicity but word of mouth made it successful enough to plan another for this August. It is being held at St. Lucy's, either outside in the plaza that was once the site of buildings 92 and 94, or in its community center. Many more people plan to attend this one.

I have made contact with this year's organizers by phone. For most there was a little confusion as to who I was, but they all knew my oldest sister. All welcomed my interest in their efforts, even though they were disappointed I would not be able to attend.

I will send a donation to help their efforts. I will pass the word to those I can that I believe have not heard. And on the 16th of August I will make the toast "to the survivors known and those unknown, whether they are remembered or whether they are not." And after the toast I will spill a little wine off the top for those who did not survive life in the War Zone.

References

Comparison between 1960 and 1980 Newark and Phoenix population rank and density by the U.S. Census Bureau.

www.census.gov/population/www/documentation/twps0027/tab19.txt
www.census.gov/population/www/documentation/twps0027/tab21.txt

"Newark was hamstrung by a number of trends in the post-WWII era. The Federal Housing Administration redlined virtually all of Newark, preferring to back up mortgages in the white suburbs."

Online Reference   http://www.answers.com/topic/newark-new-jersey?cat=travel, under Wikipedia/Newark headline

"The Newark's application for the Model Cities program in 1966 "described over 40,000 of the city's 136,000 housing units as substandard or dilapidated".

(Report for Action 1968 page 55) Online reference:
http://blog.nj.com/ledgernewark/2007/06/report_for_action.html

"Slumlords collected rent but often failed to perform regular maintenance, let alone improvements, to their properties."

(The Tenement Landlord by George Sternlieb, Rutgers University Press, Piscataway, 1969)

"There were 227 fires during the 1967 Newark Riot." "There were 9971 fires in Newark in 1972." "Sometimes landlords simply set fire to their property in hope of receiving an insurance windfall. Between 1961 and 1967 Newark averaged 3620 structural fires per year."

(From Riot to Recovery: Newark After Ten Years- Compiled and edited by Stanley B. Winters University Press, Washington, 1979:5)   Online Reference:
www.67riots.rutgers.edu/n_index.htm

"Seventh Avenue was notoriously devastated by urban renewal efforts during the 1950s." "By their proximity to I-280, the Christopher Columbus Homes became a highly visible advertisement of Newark's poverty."

On line Reference:
http://en.wikipedia.org/wiki/Seventh_Avenue,_Newark,_New_Jersey

When We Were Young and Just Knew No Better

By George Langston Cook
September 14, 2001

The brothers and I were sitting out in the sun
Laughing and a joking and justa having fun
Talking bout some of the good old memories
Of just how good the times use to be
When we were young and just knew no better

Tricycles, bicycles and little red wagons
Riding them all without having to hold on
Not a care, not a penny, it didn't seem to matter
Just trying hard to be the best softball batter
When we were young and just knew no better

Mornings hanging from things that were too high
Trying real hard to make someone else cry
Running to the house when our mothers did call
Before an afternoon of playing ball
When we were young and just knew no better

And seeing the smiles on all of our young faces
From the simple thrills of running foot races
Being in the park all throughout the day
Without running out of fun games to play
When we were young and just knew no better

Punchball and kickball in the McKinley playground
Play Hide and Seek, and being the last one found
Jump rope, and Tag, and Catch One Catch All
We also played Red Rover and a lot of Dodgeball
When we were young and just knew no better

Threw Star Pimple balls to find the best arms
chewed Bazooka gum and ate the candy Charms
Played with marbles, and yo-yo's, and spinning tops
And stole cookies from the store named Pops
When we were young and just knew no better

We slid down Bums Alley on a box of cardboard
Large enough to carry the whole hoard
Then in the back halls where we all mellowed out
And argued baseball heroes with the most clout
When we were young and just knew no better

A super hero identity each one of us had
Special powers we picked to make us all glad
I became Cyclops because of my crossed eyes
Whose optic ray blast destroyed the bad guys
When we were young and just knew no better

There was a Hulk, Mighty Thor, and a Hawkeye too
And a Captain America to lead the whole crew
We were banded together and called the Avengers
And then we kept the playground from all dangers
When we were young and just knew no better

But now these are just old memories
About the way we remember it to be
The days are gone when life was carefree
And all of us have responsibilities
Jobs, concerns, and our own families
But it's good to look back to days when we

Were young and just knew no better

Some Got Out Of There Just In Time
By George Langston Cook 7/08/08

there is much to say of the old neighborhood
not all of it pretty, not all of it good
where management did not do all that it should
and good people there did not all that they could
so some got out of there just in time

many residents of this inner city place
before it turned into a damn disgrace
left, moved out, or went away in a race
before it became more than they could face
some got out of there just in time

it once was a place that so many called home
a place worth remembering in song and poem
a place in which residents found it safe to roam
and outsiders were kept outside of its dome
but some had to get out of there just in time

some left before gunshots rang out
some left before the morality drought
some left before good living was in doubt
before losing what living there was all about
so some got out of there just in time

they left before young girls turned to hags
as boy-like men gave them small plastic bags
filled with drugs that put their minds in a gag
and turned they bodies into that of old nags
some got out of there just in time

some left before infection with project grime
that made so many boys follow a life of crime
so wherever they went they deposited a slime
that turned people touched into less than prime
so some got out of there just in time

some were chased out by their own tragedy
or something bad happened to their family
some of them moved for they wanted to be
safe in the place of their residency
some got out of there just in time

some who left waxed with fortune and fame
some found success without playing the game
some got saved and their lives became tame
some just got away to escape the shame
so some got out of there just in time

then were we who were there at the end
who were also around when it all did begin
for this place was nice when we all lived within
and this complex was like a world without sin
so some got out of there just in time

they closed down the buildings for several years
and court fights produced for us very few cheers
the city won the right that brought some to tears
to tear down the place that some once held dear
before they got out of there just in time

there were some who waited until the very last
who lived around the buildings until before the blast
of course they were of the homeless or junkie class
who used Columbus to cover their ass
and had to be thrown out just in time

but now to say something for the rest of us
we did not leave early and our lives did not bust
what we witnessed there made our living perilous
but we stayed until Columbus returned to the dust
some got out of there just in time

yes we saw how a good place turned bad
knowing that the things we lost makes us mad
having memories provoking our feelings so glad
about how we grew up in the hood that we had
and if there are more memories I just have to add
it's the loss of friends and times that make us feel sad

then we all got out of there just in time

WAR STORIES

There is a war going on out there, and if you are not careful it will catch up to you and anyone important in your life. I found out about it years ago, but I had no idea just how dangerous it was. Let me tell you that it is not a war in the conventional sense with armies and weapons. But, there is an enemy, winners and losers, and the innocents that suffer because that is the nature of this war.

The stories I'm about to tell you are all true. Names have been changed to protect those of the guilty that are still alive. If what I leave you with does not change your attitude and the behavior of your reckless brothers and sisters, then their death will be on your hands.

I spent most of my formative years in a city that was the most densely populated in this country. The block I lived on had only sixteen buildings; each one twelve stories high excluding the lobby, and had eight apartments on each floor. This apartment I lived in had three bedrooms, a living room, an eat-in kitchen, and a bathroom. Only the lobby apartments had more rooms.

This was a family community. Most apartments housed at least one child along with parents. My home consisted of seven children, two parents, and a dog, all in a small five-room apartment. And my family was not the largest in this complex. To simplify this, just think, sixteen hundred apartments, with an average of five residents each, living on a single city block that was not much larger than 4 acres. That gives each resident less than an eight by eight-foot square for elbowroom at ground level.

Cows in Wyoming have miles of room, and I've seen lawns surrounding office buildings larger than this block I called home. The priorities of life are mixed up in the war. Understand that I am not complaining because I had a lot of fun in this environment. But many of my friends died without getting a chance to see the better side of it all.

Theirs are the stories of this war.

Ronald

Young boys tend to play games of war. They will get into snowball fights in the winter, and in warmer weather they will throw rocks and bottles. We use to throw dirt bombs too, that would break into harmless grains of dirt and mud. It was fun then, and I guess to many youngsters of today, it still is.

In 1961, May 9th to be exact, Ronald and some other youngsters were playing a game of war. According to the rules by which we would play, the weapons could only be those dirt bombs that contained no slivers of glass or any rocks. To be sure we did not want to start any fights because we were all friends. One little boy, however, did not really understand the game, or the rules we played by. So, he picked up an empty Coca-Cola bottle and threw it. The bottle was one of those 28 ounce size bottles made from that heavy green glass being used at that time. The projectile hit Ronald in the neck. First, Ronald fell down from the impact, but when he saw the blood gush from his neck, he got up and tried to run for his home. He could not catch his breath, and he fell once again not more than twenty feet from the entrance to his building.

I remember this so well because at the time Ronald was eight years old and my best friend. My 9th birthday was exactly two weeks away. The little boy that threw the bottle was only five.

I remember the newspaper article's title; "Boy 5 Kills 8 Year Old." Yes, Ronald died. The bottle cut his juggler veins. When the Emergency Squad arrived at the scene, they tried desperately to stop the bleeding. They may have been successful at saving his life if they had noticed that the blood was gurgling, and air bubbles were escaping too. You see the weight of the bottle also broke Ronald's windpipe. He never really had a chance. He expired after about ten or fifteen minutes.

So yes, even young boys can die, and the youngest can kill. Do you know what your children, and young brothers and sisters are doing out there.

David

Have you ever heard of the game of "Chicken"? It is played when some one dares you to do something that you would not normally try because of the danger. It's like driving down a one way street the wrong way, putting a quarter on your forearm after the coin had been sitting in an open flame, or the more dangerous version, "Russian Roulette." The roulette game is played with a revolver that has one bullet in one of the chambers. The object of the game is to put the gun to your head and pull the trigger. If you are lucky, since the chances are in your favor, you will get one of the empty chambers.

About one year after Ronald died, David tried his hand at this roulette game once. He played along with some friends on the porch of one of the buildings during their lunch break from school. I was walking back to school when I saw David spin the chambers and put his life on the front line. He must have been lucky then.

We all knew David was no dummy... at least he got very good grades in school. It seems though that he was not as smart as we thought. On my way home from school that afternoon, I saw the flashing lights of an ambulance where I had seen David playing earlier. When I went to investigate as most of the other kids did, all I saw was the building janitor washing away blood on the sidewalk. No David anywhere. When I asked about what happened, someone said some sixth grade boy who had played hooky for the first time that afternoon, put a gun to his head and pulled the trigger.

There are many other kids, who for the sake of a little excitement will play games of chicken. Imagine that... David, age eleven, honor roll student, dead. Once again I ask, do you really know what the youth are doing? Do you care enough to give them more reasonable alternatives? In the case of Ronald, maybe the five year old did not completely understand the ramifications of his act. David on the other hand, took a calculated risk and he lost his life. He gambled in a war where even the innocents lose.

Russell

No one really knows for sure what happened to Russell. I had almost forgotten him; it had been so long ago. He was a funny guy, and would hit me on the top of my head with his school books, just to find out how hard-headed I could be. Through that though, there is a good feeling about his memory, and a nagging suspicion that nothing in the projects seemed the same after his tragic death. There were no drugs or gunplay involved, yet his end was violent.

Russell had been sent away by his family for a few weeks vacation, and he took his bicycle along with him. One day while on his vacation, he went riding and never returned. His body was found days later in a ravine, and the bike lay nearby bent beyond recognition and repair. Whoever hit him could have called someone but didn't. Evidently it took a while for him to die, as his wounds immobilized and incapacitated him, but loss of blood and dehydration were the immediate causes of death. Or was his death really caused by some uncaring individual concerned only about his insurance rates, and not the life of the boy he destroyed.

Russell left behind parents and a sister. I can see him in my mind now, young and strong, always smiling, tough, friendly, and proud… Russell, age twelve, found dead, another casualty of the war.

Gary

Gary and his sisters moved into my neighborhood sometime after Ronald died. We became fast friends, and he pulled me out of more fights than I care to remember. He was a much better fighter than I was, faster on his feet, and a lot of fun to be around. He thought, though, that hanging around the crowd I did was kind of boring. We only played safe games, like handball, around the world, relay races…you know…light stuff. He needed a little more danger, so he started hanging with the tough guys.

Most of the tough guys were not really bad, but they took chances my crowd wouldn't. They played hooky, got into gang fights, and smoked cigarettes... things tough guys did in those days for a thrill. Before Gary got to the eighth grade, he started trying to get more of a euphoric rush. Like the others in his new crowd, he began sniffing glue, and quickly progressed to inhaling things like Cabona – a fabric cleaner, drinking wine, and the new craze in the neighborhood...dope.

Heroin was not really new. We had been getting lectured about it for the past few years in school. Some folks just had to try it anyway, despite hearing it would give you a bad habit, make you steal for it, and then kill you if you did too much of it.

Now, Gary did not use too much, and he did not have a habit to my knowledge. One night though, some of the tough guys, Gary among them, went to buy some dope. They did not know the seller. To be sure, they did not know what they were buying. They gave up the money they had roughed away from some other kids and bought the product. Gary, being the leader he was, took the first shot. He quickly doubled over. Soon he began to change color, from the rich black of most of his family to a kind of cross between a purplish tint and ash white. Everyone panicked and left him there. The next day he was found dead with rat poison in his veins.

Drug dealers do not clear their product with the Food and Drug Administration for its safety and purity. They are only accountable to their own greed. Some guys will do anything for a dollar, like sell rat poison to a youth or anyone else trying to buy illegal drugs. Can you really be sure of what you are getting when what you want is illegal? Ask Gary!

Antonio

One of the most important things in life is the communication between friends. We all need it, much like water, food, shelter, and the air we breathe. It is just that important to good health and well being. Without it there is but emotional pain and suffering, and no desire for life.

Antonio was a friend of one of my younger brothers. By the time he was twelve years old, he thought he had discovered his one true love. The only problem with this is that the girl he loved did not love him, and perhaps did not even like him.

Antonio felt this rejection from her and took it to heart. If he had used his friends to talk about his feelings, they probably laughed at him or something like that since young teenagers can be quite insensitive to anything except for their own desires. Antonio's father had been dead for some time, and he had no older brother to help him through this stage of life. And even though he spent a lot of time with my brother in my house, I could not tell how much this non-affair affected Antonio.

One night, Antonio took a walk along the highway behind the complex to contemplate his feelings for this girl, and to evaluate the meaning of love as he knew it. The sound of cars and trucks must have given him the answers he sought because Antonio jumped in front of the biggest, fastest moving vehicle available. He was dragged about an eighth of a mile underneath a speeding eighteen wheeler. His crushed body parts could not be reconstructed well enough to resemble the young man at his funeral.

Antonio left behind his mother, two sisters, and a younger brother, not to mention many shocked friends that could not admit to themselves they saw his suffering. Are you sensitive enough to recognize his symptoms in your friends and loved ones? In order to win the battles of this war, you must be.

Boobie

I had known Boobie since the first few days after I moved into the projects a week after my fourth birthday. I am still on good terms with his family that is still alive. Though it was true he never did hang out with the group of guys I did, we all knew him as one of the fellas.

About the same time Gary met with his demise, Boobie began to experiment with life on the wild side. He took chances so that he could get the things his family could not and would not provide. First, it was harmless, stealing candy from the local merchants, but his habit grew to become a much bigger headache for the neighborhood. By his early teenage years, he was snatching pocketbooks from ladies coming out of stores on Broadway and Downtown, and he was getting caught.

First, Boobie was sent to the Youth House, then to one of those kind of places that makes tough guys tougher and bad little thieves into worse thieves. He came out not only to rob again, but also to get addicted to drugs. Eventually, he made his way into one of those methadone treatment programs. Those programs were designed to get addicts off of heroin, and to maintain their habits with methadone, a synthetic drug. Most of the people on these programs found no cure for their habits, and Boobie was no exception.

One night while being "maintained", Boobie drank a large volume of vodka. The combination put him into a coma. He recovered, but that is how his life was going. On the same day his father died, Boobie was found dead in his bathtub. Maybe he slipped and bumped his head, maybe it was a relapse into a coma, maybe it was due to drugs, but those who knew him best say the loss of his father was too much for Boobie to take. A few days after that, his nephew died too.

It's hard to think of a worse family tragedy in the neighborhood...the father dead, the nephew also, both of natural causes, and Boobie....cause of death unknown...a victim of the risks he took in the war.

Michael

You may believe that people reap what they sow, and that might even be true. But again, there may be underlying reasons why some boys become bad. And maybe the outcome of a day can be changed through the use of good judgement and free will.

Michael was wild and uncontrollable. He was a thief, and he was addicted to drugs that affected his surface personality negatively. But deep down inside, Michael had the capacity for true friendship.

Michael's life was taken by his mother's paramour, shot down while he was in a fit of anger, threatening death himself, and wreaking havoc in their home. Tragic though it was, no one in the family appears to be sorry. There are no pictures of him, nor any evidence of his existence on display at the homes of his mother or sister. But I remember him anyway.

Michael could be sober, and he could be a lot of fun, but instead he is dead. He never seemed as bad to me as he did to others. I had known him since he was born, and now he is gone. I can only wonder if there had been no drugs in the neighborhood, and if there had been more love in his life, what would have Michael become, other than just another casualty of the war.

Paulie

I never expected Paulie to turn out the way he did. He came from a religious family. His mother attended (and still attends) church services regularly, and avoided drink and curse. Paulie himself seemed quiet enough, friendly, and stayed out of trouble with the people in the neighborhood. He often came into my mother's home. He respected her and all womanhood in general. I never saw him or knew him to be under the influence of any drug, and he seemed sober minded. He hardly appeared to be Michael's younger brother.

But Paulie had a dark side he kept well hidden. He was a ruthless robber, and wasted no time on little stickups or strong-arm jobs. He went after banks. He committed a series of bank holdups both near the projects here and somewhere in Texas. After FBI agents cornered him, Paulie took a family hostage before the Feds took him into custody. He is doing Federal time now.

Who would have thought that cute, little Paulie had such malevolence in his heart, or that someone could hide it so well. Was it the money, or was it the thrill of the chase? The war breeds such soldiers, capable of deceit, filled with hatred, and seething with violence. Paulie, it seems turned out to be one of them.

Eddie Junior

Eddie's story is truly a family tragedy. To my knowledge he had no fear, and conducted his life as if whatever the consequences of his actions, he could handle it. He had three sisters that in many ways were just like him. From the beginning they were fighters, obviously a family trait. To fight one of them was to fight them all. They never accepted defeat, not physically, not mentally. That was their family strength, and it was also their weakness.

There was nothing Eddie and his sisters seemed afraid to try…fighting anyone, playing hooky, engaging in crime, and getting high on drugs. They were almost inseparable in habit as they were in life. It is different now that Eddie is dead.

Now I am not exactly sure how Eddie died for there are many different accounts of his legend, but I do know something. His sisters remained behind in living their lives with much of the family spirit and habits. Their bodies lost their natural beauty and the pride of their Black womanhood eroded. Though they remained fighters striving to preserve their individual and family honor, they lost a lot more often. Men manhandled them publicly and dishonored them; men Eddie could have eaten for lunch.

One by one they died. First to go was the youngest, Diane, while giving birth. The middle girl, Celestine, went next horribly addicted, diseased, and abused. And the eldest Queen Esther hung on for years in battered relationships, homeless, and alone before she just faded away. They remained loyal to each other, and its funny that we became better friends as they each approached their end.

I can not help myself from believing that had it not been for Eddie's death, and their narcotics use, they could have achieved almost anything. Their family traits, aggressive family pride, togetherness, tenacity, and their unwillingness to accept defeat is the basic stuff success is made of. Instead, they became just another set of victims in the war.

Tommy

They tell me Tommy died when he fell from the subway platform in front of a moving subway car in New York City. I remember seeing him sometimes, his eyes barely open, his clothes in disarray as he struggled to maintain his composure because he was so high. For me, it didn't matter what he was high on because whatever it was, it was destroying one of the best basketball players in the neighborhood. He had good moves and a sharp shooting eye. All of that is wasted now.

When I returned home in 1985, I ran into one of Tommy's old coaches while I substituted at Webster. The coach reminisced just how well Tommy played the game. He wondered what had happened to Tommy, what college he went to. I did not want to say he died and how he did, because I didn't want someone else to know how our neighborhood could claim so many worthwhile lives, and convert their bodies to carrion unfit for vultures and rats to dine on. I did not want him to know how someone like Tommy could change so much. Somehow, I believe the coach knew anyway.

Although drugs were not the immediate cause of his untimely demise, it's almost a sure thing that Tommy was high when he died. I miss him, but that began long before the train hit him. I began to miss him when I saw him change, when the drugs first overpowered him, when he could no longer maintain his cool for that is when Tommy really died.

Jesse,
The Last of the Jenkins Boys

The Jenkins' boys, Foots, Horace, Gordon, Jesse, and Tommy shared many characteristics. All possessed a high degree of athletic skill. All possessed an outgoing personality that most often displayed itself in the form of comedy. They all mixed sociably with others.

"Foots" was the first giant person I knew yet his height was never a threat.   Despite his great size, gentleness and clowning characterized him.   He completely disarmed people with his humor.   Gordon lacked his eldest brother's physical stature, but settled on being funnier, much funnier.   He excelled as a comedian, heads and shoulders above his brother.   Whether telling a joke or creating a story, Gordon mimicked the voice, age, and sex of the characters he made up.   We thought he could perform professionally.   Tommy, the youngest possessed the best athletic talent of his brothers.   Each of the three stood out in the neighborhood like the brightest stars in the night sky.   All three died before fulfilling their greatest potential.

Jesse, aged between Tommy and Gordon, survives, and his success highlights the character of all his family members.   Jesse represents the last of the men from a generation in his family.   He always exhibited a flair for academia and self discipline from an early age. He contented himself with athletic competence, instead of relying on sport as a way out of the neighborhood.   He listened and laughed to his brothers' joking rather than competing with it.   He went to college quietly, and performed his studies privately.   He completed law school, and became a member of the state bar, silently.   He serves the community admirably.

Norman

I saw him as a hero.   In my youth I admired and respected him. Who could blame me for looking up to Norman?   He possessed bravery and strength.   He exhibited all around athletic prowess from his earliest days through high school.   All the sports he played, he did so well, and he mastered many football positions in high school.   His daring exploits on the field of play were almost legendary.   In addition, he was nearly a straight A student, and sang like a bird.   He bullied no one, and backed down to no challenges or conflicts others may have tried to confront him with.   He charmed with a smile, cool wit, and his good-hearted friendly manner.   I always considered him to be a friend, and he treated me as if I was one of his.

He changed. Use of heroin and methadone made him look puffed up like the Pillsbury Doughboy. He walked the street, often looking like a bum and panhandling. He let himself down. His potential for success became stifled. It is almost as if he were not deserving of my youthful admiration.

I've heard many explanations as to what happened to Norman, and any one of the stories could be true. I was once told he went to college but only lasted for a semester, where he found out he was not the standout superstar he was in high school, but only one of many such luminaries. I then heard he became a father early on, and that cut his college career short, as well as a rewarding future based on completing college and perhaps professional football fame. I even heard he put his life on the back burner to take on the responsibilities of supporting the wife and children of one of his fallen comrades from the projects. It even could have been an injury that ended his playing career early. It could have been anything. It doesn't even seem to matter any more, since he died several years ago of a heart attack. He did not make it to 45.

Was it the pressure of society, a lack of self-confidence, or the inability to pass by the challenge of drug abuse that destroyed him? Or was he really a coward, unable to face the rigors of adult life after the excitement of high school athletic success died down. Whatever the reason, Norman is just another casualty of the war we face in life.

Keith

Keith and I started kindergarten and graduated high school together. We shared friendship and many friends. Our families were close. We spent many days and evenings at each other's homes. We competed in many areas, and sometimes rubbed each other the wrong way. He teased me a lot, so we fought as well as played together.

Keith could run like the wind, and played basketball better than most of our friends. A group of us would run to the Boys' Club regularly, and Keith always arrived first, a good two minutes before the next runner hit the door. By his sophomore year in high school, he had become one of the state's premier cross-country runners, and ran a mile in close to 4-minute time. And his basketball game exceeded his track potential. By his senior year, he averaged scoring in the high twenties, and jumped the game's opening tip off, although he played the guard position.

He definitely possessed college level athletic ability, and the stuff to make professional basketball dreams come true. He became very popular, a star, but this popularity led him to a fashionable lifestyle. He gained access to and used cocaine while he was still in high school, even though it would be years before it was readily available for sale in the neighborhood.

Cocaine destroyed Keith's desire to run track. He left college before the end of his first semester. Without playing college ball in those days meant no possibility of professional ball-playing career. As a result, he lost the potential of earning millions as a basketball player. He landed a job at the Post Office, but lost that job too due to his drug habit. He eventually became a bartender.

Keith eventually died by the time he was 36, supposedly due to AIDS. He used drugs as a sign of momentary success. His athleticism gave him fleeting moments of fame based on achievement rather than on character. Together, they destroyed great potential in Keith.

Jay Jay

From the beginning, Jay-Jay had a lot to overcome. His oldest sister possessed only marginal intellect. Today, we would call her mentally challenged, but as kids, we said she was just plain retarded. We teased him and encouraged him at the same time. He tried so hard to hang out with us on the basketball court until he learned and grew to outplay many of us, despite him being several years younger.

He has a lot to overcome again. He gave himself the name "Mr. Machine" to describe his scoring ability, but now he walks the streets in a mechanical gait. He talks o himself, stares almost catatonically, and often smells of alcohol and feces. He may

83

remember your name long enough to ask for an odd amount of change or a cigarette, although he doesn't smoke.

He is shot out. And it's hard to believe at his height, he scored points like a machine, averaging more than 35 points a game in Division III college basketball, and tried out for the New York Knicks as a walk on after failing to get drafted.

Billy

Billy died in a pool of his own blood with a hypodermic needle lodged in his arm. They found him alone in his room with the door locked from the inside, after the stench of his rotting corpse alerted others of his condition days following the event. He had such promise. He possessed a fine mind, and excelled in school work. He lacked athleticism but that really didn't matter. People liked him, and he came from a good family. Who knows what it was that gave him the trouble with himself? Maybe trying to be the man of the house when he was still just a boy had something to do with it.

Pete

Pete was one of the older guys in the neighborhood, and lived in my building. He studied the martial arts for years under the tutelage of the local expert, and he became quite good at it. I will always remember the fear he instilled in others, and the respect he deserved and received. Now, he is dead of a drug overdose, leaving behind a wife and children who were cared for by his friend Norman. In the wake of his death, and the manner in which it occurred, Pete became nothing to fear or respect, and he wasted years of discipline.

Walter and Andre

Fate and coincidence may define how two lives can change forever after meeting at one point in space and time. To me, that describes what happened between Walter and Andre.

Walter stayed in trouble most of his life. Many people saw him as a tough guy, incorrigible and just plain bad. I think he was more unfortunate than bad. Life never gave him a break. He was my friend, a good friend.

Walter and I started school together, and from the beginning trouble found him. He seemed disobedient to authority in the first grade because he'd go to the bathroom whether or not the teacher gave him permission or not. We discovered later he had a weak bladder condition, but by then, negative perceptions about his character were already set in stone. Later, in trying to show his manhood, he acted up a lot, started fights, teased girls in class, and stole.

Walter's father was in jail most of Walter's life. Before we graduated from the ninth grade Walter spent time in the Youth House, Jamesburg, and Annandale, following in his father" footsteps. He spent most of his teen years institutionalized, and wasted away even more years in jail than out during his twenties. He committed mostly petty crimes against property and suffered from substance abuse. Walter's reputation from his youth carried all the bad luck he ever needed, but he received more… much more.

We called Andre "the giant." He stood over six foot seven inches tall and weighed nearly two hundred pounds. He played basketball for one of the local high schools but went no further, mostly because he was awkward. He was a relatively nice guy on and off the court. Despite his great size he normally bullied no one. He failed however to live up to his athletic desires, which created great frustration in him, and changed his life forever.

Andre began by smoking marijuana, but eventually graduated to a combination of codeine and barbiturates, known commonly as "hits" or "Cibas and syrup."

You could easily tell if someone was high off hits because their eyelids were half closed, their hands constantly wiped away slob coming from the corners of their mouth, and they always seemed about ready to fall over forward with a near terminal lean. This drug combination created an euphoric effect resembling the heroin high, and added a false sense of courage. In this state, people behaved aggressively as if no harm would befall them.

One day while under the influence of hits, Andre harassed Walter. Walter had at that time been released from jail for about six months, and was making every effort to remain out of trouble. Andre persisted. Walter turned around and punched the much bigger man in the jaw. Drugged as he was, Andre lost his balance, fell, and busted his head on the concrete curb near the corner of Summer and Seventh avenues.

Was fate responsible for Andre picking Walter to harass? Was coincidence the cause of his head hitting the curb? We may never know for sure, but what we do know is that Andre died from the injury, and Walter returned to jail, this time for involuntary manslaughter. The war took one life to incarcerate another.

In his late thirties when he got out of jail, Walter was unemployable, institutionalized, and undereducated for life in the late eighties and early nineties. I saw him often trying to survive by selling drugs on Seventh Avenue in front of the now emptied Columbus Homes. Sometimes he slept at his mother's apartment, but often he crept into one of the vacated project buildings. From time to time I'd bring him a plate, a needed care package, bus fare, or invited him to just some friendly conversation in my apartment. He died several years ago.

The Stewart Trilogy
Bruce, Clyde, and Gerald

Bruce was the oldest and my best friend's godfather. He benefited from strong parental guidance, a hardworking father in the household, and years of parochial school education two generations before it became fashionable in the Black neighborhood. He possessed both faith and conviction. He received training for the ministry, was thoughtful, friendly, and protective. To my knowledge Bruce still lives today, though only God knows how and why.

Bruce possessed a rage, uncontrollably at times, and very few people in their right minds stood up to his anger and penchant for violence. He survived multiple gunshot and stab wounds, incarcerations, and addiction. He delved into serious crime, and had been known to pull stick-ups on his family and people who knew him as if daring them to seek retribution. He intimidated many others from the bricks.

Yes, he is lucky to be alive. Bruce has done his time, and no doubt in my mind probably deserves more. With all he has gone through, the strength of his family, and the benefit of education, it seems he had not learned from his mistakes. His care of others is transitional, and likes to have things his way. More than likely his end will be violent, for that is how he had lived hive life... as a walk on the wild side.

If Clyde played second fiddle to anyone, it was his brother Bruce. They looked and acted like bookends, both short, block-shaped, solid, and strong. He was wild and aggressive, an alcoholic also addicted to other drugs, a stick up artist, and a rowdy. Clyde is dead now. Alcohol and other drugs and the consequential physical diseases ended his life. He left behind several children who should hopefully learn from their father's mistakes.

I went to Clyde's funeral and to his home afterwards to touch bases with a family I've known most of my life. Bruce took his brother's death so hard he caused a ruckus and was forcibly removed from there down to Green Street. Their father wished aloud that he knew how he as a parent could have produced such sons. I told Mr. Stewart to blame the pressures of the old neighborhood. Perhaps the untimely death of their mother, his subsequent remarriage to the second Mrs. Stewart, and how his sons chose to respond to the two situations also played a part. He had given his sons love and understanding, a superior education, and indomitable spirits. Both Bruce and Clyde could have very easily used those gifts for good, instead of letting grief, peer pressure, and drugs turn them into tools for evil.

A few years younger than Bruce and Clyde, Gerald possessed their same uninhibited ferocity. Some folk say he lacked any kind of moral character. He intimidated others by acting crazy, fighting, and engaging in criminal activities, but all that fades away when I think of the last time I saw him during the 70's.

Some idiot employed as an armed security guard at Columbus walked up to me in the Community Center for some unknown reason pulled out his gun, put it to my head, cocked the hammer and said "I want to see you dance." Gerald happened to see what was going on. As I was doing some kind of shuffle, Gerald walked up to the security guard and whispered something in his ear that I could not hear. The guard took the gun from my temple, holstered it, and left the premises as fast as his legs could move him. From that day on, I cannot remember ever seeing that guard again. So I thank Gerald, the so called crazy man with no moral principles or good sense for getting me out of an untenable situation.

Throughout most of the eighties and early nineties, I understand Gerald remained in one of the state's maximum security institutions for a violent crime. For a man that to my knowledge did not get a chance to finish high school, he gained a bit of a reputation as an excellent jailhouse lawyer, applying these skills to help others as well as himself on appeals and parole applications. They say he never lost his aggressive nature and may be capable of killing if paroled. He did eventually gain his freedom, getting out of jail on parole, and tried to apply his legal skills in the paralegal profession. In this Gerald failed. He went through that part of his life beaten down, addicted, a lifelong felon, unable to make the transition to society.

Just as I would for Bruce of Clyde if he were alive, I would give whatever I had to see Gerald free and able to use his many gifts to benefit society. We all have lost something wonderful because the Stewart boys fell as victims of the war.

Bernard

Bernard went to Howard University, where he fell from a four story window while smoking a joint. He broke both of his legs and arms, his back, his neck, and slept for two weeks in a coma. He awoke paralyzed from the neck down and the experts said he'd never walk again. After seventy two days in traction he moved his toes. After almost eight months of rehabilitation he walked with a cane. He now walks and runs without any outside assistance…the only evidence of his ordeal is a barely noticeable limp. His only failure was refusing to let someone else's doubts stop his progress. He had his beliefs to sustain him and left the experience with a stronger sense of God.

Bernard overcame that life and death struggle but the eighties and nineties brought new trials and tribulations into his life in the form of a girl, a girl named Cocaine. Bernard fell victim to the seductress after securing a decent position with the City. This hussy damn near stole from him everything he ever worked for. He lost the loving relationship he had with his wife. He forfeited his home and a small store he owned and operated. He gave up much of the respect he gained from his first ordeal, all behind the ravages of that girl, Cocaine.

But Bernard had something in him, something greater than the lure of cocaine, and he fought back with it. Bernard reattached himself to his faith, his belief in God, and put up a battle with addiction to make us proud. At last look, Bernard had several years clean, was working for the city, and moving forward after so many again had given his soul up for lost.

Bruce

Not long after the death of my mother, Bruce was shot dead by three teenage punks outside of a store near Springfield Avenue following an argument that took place inside. They had to shoot, first because they were punks, secondly because Bruce would have kicked their butts if they hadn't. You see, Bruce was trained by his father in karate, and was by all accounts capable of reaching mastery had not drugs interfered with his life. He was barely in his early 30's.

Long had it been since his family moved from Columbus, but somehow he developed along the same lines of our old neighborhood, or maybe it was an affliction that was really city-wide.

89

Found Dead

Some men I grew up with were found dead in apartments, motel rooms, or some isolated location long after they died. The odor from their decaying bodies alerted outsiders to where they were. Somehow, their lives shared more than the way we found out about their endings.

Whether we speak of David, Lorenzo, or Dennis, while their personalities seemed miles apart, they had similar experiences. David seemed to have a dark spirit. He seldom hid his criminal mentality brought on by his drug use. As a youth he played well with others, though he probably took a little more ribbing because he was his family's youngest. Drugs and crime played heavily in his lifestyle. He spent his teens and twenties in and out of lock ups. For many years I never knew his whereabouts until his body turned up in a New York City apartment weeks after he died.

Lorenzo "Poochie" also seemed the dark and brooding type. Years younger than both Dennis and David, he seemed to have the toughest time at life. He came from a very large family that lived in a lobby apartment. Though drugs played a part of his problems, so was it true of his need to be a tough guy. He put some time behind bars and searched for redemption. He never seemed to get it together on the outside.

The last time I saw Poochie alive, he was entering the Mt. Carmel Guild rehab program shortly after a release from incarceration. As we spoke on the corner of University Avenue and James Street he expressed strongly that he was tired the way his life was going. He hoped the program could help him. I wished him well, and invited him over if he could make it. I never saw him again.

When his body was found and identified, its condition shocked and disturbed many of those who knew him. Lorenzo's end came violently, though it is difficult imagining who could get the upper hand on him.

Dennis also came from a large family and seemed fun to be around for the most part. He cracked jokes and toyed with folks more

90

than David or Lorenzo would tolerate. He most often had pep in his step, a smile on his face and a gleam in his eye. He married a lovely Ms Wendy and all seemed fine and dandy for several years.

Dennis' fall came as the scourge of crack cocaine made its rounds in the neighborhood. As a result of his relationship with it he ended up incarcerated like David but for only a few years. He gained his freedom and returned home amid hoopla and great expectations. They did not last. The word came that Dennis was found dead and so badly decomposed his casket was closed at the wake. As with David no violence was known to cause his end. How strange that must be for war victims.

Big Willie

Willie was a few years older than me and lived in our building on the eleventh floor. His relative round stature belied his physical prowess. He didn't really act tough but he was fast and agile. He'd box around with those of us willing to give him a go, and he notoriously punched us hard in the chest if he saw us smoking cigarettes or trying to be too cool. Here he was trying to keep us from smoking years before the Surgeon General's warning appeared on any cigarette packs.

Willie fell hard into the drug life, right around the time I went into the service. For years, he terrorized some people to get his daily dose. Willie was eventually murdered as he sat in a barber's chair on Hawthorne Avenue.

Dickie

I understand some negative things have been said about Mr. Smith by one of the other memoirs written by a past Columbus Homes denizen. Surely, by many standards he could be considered a truly bad person, but I see him differently than I did when we were younger.

I remember meeting and being afraid of Dickie in my earliest school grades yet don't recall him in school much after that. Dickie owned excellent hand skills, fought a lot, and perhaps challenged teachers and some of us students more than what was acceptable. He ended up early in life going to the Youth House, and a few other places. He gained more of a reputation for fighting than for his drug use. The drug use put him in situations of homelessness, the loss of some of his digits, attempts at treatment and God knows what else.

But Dickie is still alive through it all and keeps fighting on. He has suffered the tragic death of his son, decades of addiction, and methadone treatment. And he is still around fighting on to live with the heart of a champion. Despite all of his downfalls, how life has continuously knocked him down, he keeps getting up.

Maybe his standard of living does not measure up to yours or mine, but I wonder how we may have fared walking a few miles in his shoes. Would our hearts measured up to his.

Dickie Epilogue

Dickie was found in his apartment two years ago. He died alone, quietly and peacefully, succumbing to one of the infirmities of this world, diabetes or some other ailment. His fighting spirit stayed with him all the days of his life, never giving in to demands of surrendering information.

Glenn

Who would have thought that a man coming from such a devout background would gain his notoriety? Glenn lived in my building for several years. His parents and sisters belonged to the Jehovah Witnesses. As part of our group he wasn't that big, and not that good of a fighter. In fact another one of our group flipped him right on his noggin and knocked him out cold. Sure he had a little jump shot but it wasn't really all that.

Glenn's family moved out and the father purchased stores on the Four Corners of Hawthorne Avenue and Bergen Street. After the father's death, Glenn used those storefronts to set up one of the most lucrative drug empires on the East Coast. After years of operation out of the storefronts especially the liquor store the Feds took him down.

Funny though, that member of our old crew that flipped him on his noggin and knocked Glenn out was operating in the same area as a member of Newark's finest. I wonder...

Daryl

I knew Daryl, Chatty's younger brother almost since he was born. Though during childhood he never hung out with my crowd because of the years between us, after his brother's death, and throughout his adulthood, we got to know each other better.

We teased him a lot because his head was long and large when he was a kid. When he reached his late teen aged years, he hung out on the Avenue shooting pool, which he was very good at. He also got high with hits, very high.

I remember how early on Saturday and Sunday mornings, I would find him up at Branch Brook Park, high as hell, shooting the lights out of the baskets. He was an uncanny shooter. It didn't matter how well I tried to cover him, he would hit the shot while trash talking me all along.

Somehow he survived taking hits and became a responsible adult to a large degree. He went to work for years with a vendor down Neck, and maintained a close relationship with another good friend Najee. He lived with his mother throughout the years, and helped her financially. Drug use led to his demise.

Daryl got caught up when crack cocaine made its way through Columbus. Sometime during the eighties he lost or left his longtime employment and could be seen on Sheffield Drive running errands for the drug dealers there. He never did any serious time to my knowledge, but rehabilitation was just as far from his mind.

There needs to be something said about Daryl's heart. He produced two children while he was still involved with cocaine with the girlfriend of another close friend. That friend had separated himself from the situation temporarily with some outside assistance. When that friend sought to return to his family, Darrell remained as part of the family. To my knowledge, no conflicts occurred between Daryl and his past friend and he often took care of all the children in the household.

Daryl succumbed to a series of illnesses related to his drug use. In his last days his suffering and regrets were great, but I never heard him complain. His children are cared for together by his friend and their mother.

In living the life he did, Daryl showed his heart was bigger than his head. Beyond any of my educational accomplishments, he portrayed in many ways what humanity should be about. Maybe his trash talking about me while we played basketball was true.

Logan

Logan appeared on the basketball court wearing what appeared to be the old fashioned girls' tennis shoes and plaid short pants. It was evident he could not afford Converse All Stars which were in vogue at the time (and neither could I). Underneath many of our breaths, we laughed at him at first. As we came to know though, this relatively short, big handed, and long-armed basketball phenomenon used English on the ball while performing trick shot after trick shot, embarrassing and teaching us that it wasn't what you wore that made you a basketball player.

Logan shot, rebounded, passed, and moved with and without the ball, until we all knew that if he was out there, we wanted him on the team. Sam Clark, Pat Davis and Ron King, perhaps the best of the older guys that let us into their games as well as Jimmy Smith, Irving Chapman, and Keith Coleman all respected what Logan did on the court. He taught me a lot about the game

No one seemed to know much about Logan off the court. We did not even know how old he was, or much about where he lived besides that he was in Building 82. I once met the girl he eventually married when I was in junior college. He was not put off by the fact she only had one leg. He died of a heart attack in the middle of the 1980's.

Tank

Several years after my family moved in, Tank moved into Columbus from off the nearby side streets with his mother and brother. His cousins Hubert and Herbert were among my best friends, but Tank was another issue. At first, he did not seem so bad to me. I mean we all fought, and many times fought each other, and that was okay. Tank turned out to be downright mean. He did things my crowd did not do. He got involved in drugs and crime in big way. He pulled robberies, stick-ups, strong armed jobs that gave him quite a bad reputation, and that is even after his family moved out of the projects for "suburban" East Orange. He began doing time before he completed high school. I lost track of him but he never lost track of Columbus.

He would come back around and do his dirt, much to the dislike of many. His targets were often lesser criminals and sometimes the innocent that got in his way. When I was away either at school or in the military, I was told he stuck up one of my younger brothers in my mother's apartment. There was even a rumor that he mugged my mother in the back hall. I don't know for sure about everything else he did, he was bad, really bad.

Tank spent a lot of years in prison. It seems that while incarcerated at Rahway State Prison, he became somewhat of an inmate leader. Highly respected on the inside for his treacherous reputation on the outside, Tank used his notoriety to keeping a semblance of power and control over that inmate population.

Sometimes Tank needed some civilized contact and received it from an unlikely source, someone who may have had many reasons to hold a grudge against him, a corrections officer, my brother. I was told my brother spent many hours outside his cell reminiscing about the good and bad times of living in Columbus. They both gained a kind of respect and friendship toward each other. And that respect and friendship spread from inside those walls and encompassed my family. When my mother was on her deathbed, he came by and paid his respects.

Crime or drugs incarcerated Tank again where he became inflicted by a fatal disorder while behind the prison walls. He weakened and decayed physically to a point of near death. His brother Leroy made many appeals to the prison authorities to have him released and allowed to die at home, but was unable to gain the humanitarian released because the authorities deemed Tank a "danger to society". Many believe the real reason for the denial of early release was the prison authority's desire to punish leadership of the prison population. As a result, Tank eventually died in prison.

For a long time I held a grudge against Tank for what he had done to members of my family, but those same family members found it in their heart to forgive him for his sins against them. And now, so do I.

Leonard

Someone found Leonard dead with a spike in his arm in the back stairwell of Building 10, where he was known to provide some security for drug operations there. It was a long fall from where he was in life to where he ended.

Leonard possessed size, strength, and good athletic prowess as a youth, and benefit from parents that were secure. His father owned a small bar off Broad Street that provided a tidy income, so Leonard and his sister appeared to want for nothing.

Leonard played high school football after moving from the projects. After graduating he became a member of the Newark Police where he gained quite a reputation as a sharp shooter. In fact, he was a super cop. He married one of the loveliest ladies from the projects, and if his life ended then some would have said it was a good full life.

Leonard had a secret though, a secret that got him thrown off the police force. This is where I become a little confused. I'm unsure whether he had always messed around with drugs or whether it only occurred as cocaine began to take over the City in the late 70's and early 80's. At any rate, Leonard began sticking up drug dealers for their money and their drugs, along with my brother. Rehabilitation stopped my brother; loss of his shield failed to stop Leonard.

I saw him often in his later years, running security for KP's crew in the building where he died. Some say a falling out lead to the end of Leonard's life instead of what appeared to be an accidental overdose.

Jimmy White

I wanted to write this story for a long time but it was always very hard to start. I wanted to call it Kunta Kenta, after the African character in Alex Haley's "Roots", because we called Jimmy by that named affectionately because he was very dark skinned. He also possessed a very broad smile resembling the one that the original King Kong flashed just before he grabbed Faye Wray. African characteristics both, his dark skin color and broad smile stood out on him, although he was American born and bred.

Jimmy never wronged you, and always held up his end. His friendly manner and laughing spirit made him fun to be around. He told good jokes, made wise cracks, and provided us with plenty of good times. He hung out with us, did the things we did, and was there if you needed him. He kept a job.

Jimmy was just an okay guy, responsible, and caring too. He married a woman who already had two children. She cheated on him and eventually divorced him, but through that he still loved her and treated her kids well. Jimmy deserved better.

Jimmy rode with a friend in one of those small Korean sub-compact sized cars. A reckless driver, obviously in a hurry and almost assuredly under the influence of something, ran a red light and slammed into the passenger side of the car Jimmy was sitting in. He died on the scene, the accident's only victim. He had barely turned thirty years old.

Why waste such a young, valuable life, such a worthwhile soul? Maybe in war, what we value doesn't really matter. Then maybe again his life had purpose and meaning because he left a positive impression on those lucky enough to have known him. The old adage "the good die young" has merit in this case. Nearly twenty years later many friends remember and miss him. With his loss, we survivors have become the war's victims.

Dwayne

War claims the lives belonging to the best men of their generation before they fulfill their greatest potential. It takes the good and the bad, and it took Dwayne "Chatty" Hines, who could have been the best of us all. His story has become one of the greatest legends emanating from Columbus Homes.

Chatty (his nickname because he spoke fast and often) was short and stubby in stature, and was kind of a pushover as a youngster. One year down South changed that. He returned bigger, taller, and stronger accompanied by a bit of a mean streak and a zeal for excitement. He once beat up one of my brothers and I at the same time, striking us down with our own shoes. As embarrassing as this was, we remained friends.

We did many crazy things together. One Saturday, Chatty and I broke into the local elementary school to pull fire alarms. We sat in the back stairwells talking about any subject under the sun. Among our favorite topics was what we'd do if we had all the money in the world. We also read and collected comic books and named ourselves after our favorite comic book characters.

Chatty became the "Incredible Hulk" a brilliant yet timid scientist whom once exposed to a dose of deadly radiation became a rampaging seemingly mindless and destructive brute with amazing strength that increased the angrier he became. Chatty adapted himself to that persona completely. He wore "Incredible Hulk" tee shirts into adulthood daily. Whenever he became angry he would announce to all, "I'm the Incredible Hulk" before getting physical.

Chatty also possessed a very vivid imagination. If you asked him what he would do if Martians landed in our playground he might respond in this manner:

"First, I will offer them my hand in friendship. Should their intention prove hostile and begin shooting laser beams at me, my anger will increase exponentially. I will force my adrenaline to flow at such a rate that my strength would rival that of the Incredible Hulk. I will twirl my hands at supersonic speed creating with that motion compressed air combustion balls to throw at the creatures. Then I'd stomp my foot to the ground, opening a bottomless chasm, toss their spaceship in, and then pull the torn Earth back together..."

Chatty also seemed to be a master of the English language and used that skill to make everyone laugh. He could make up words and pull together diverse concepts in "playing the dozens" or "talking about your mother" that could have you in stitches for a week. He was truly a funny character.

Chatty also loved children. He always made himself available to the little kids in the neighborhood as their playmate and their protector. Usually a small band of kids would surround him egging him on in games of "tag" or "follow the leader" and he freely participated. He kept them positively occupied, out of trouble and as far away from drug influences as possible. Maybe he was still stuck in his own childhood, or maybe followed a higher moral calling no longer found in our neighborhood amongst the teen aged men.

Chatty was tough too, but not a tough guy. He performed acts requiring courage that even the tough guys would not attempt. He has climbed down to the ground from the top roofs without the aide of any equipment as if he were a rock climber. He leaped over moving cars, placing a hand down on their hoods as they went by. In addition, he was the first person to climb the rungs to the smoke stack, a structure adjacent to one of the buildings in the complex and almost as high. (Rumor has it that Muttsy and Pauley did it too.) Chatty was no pushover.

If Chatty had a fatal flaw it was his propensity for trouble to find him. Maybe it was an assault, or a B & E that got him sent up for a year, but when he returned he was bigger, meaner, and a little bit crazier. If he applied himself in the direction of school and sports, any football team, college or professional would have loved to have him play at linebacker. He could have been a star as a big, strong, and fast individual possessing a good blend of intelligence, intensity, and insanity. He stayed away from college though and involved himself with concerns of a more serious nature.

I returned to Columbus Homes after my military service and found Chatty on the front lines of the war at home. Drugs and petty crime lacked the strength to destroy him. It took his own pride and insanity to consume him. He feuded with some guys that moved into his building. I don't know when it started or how Chatty saw it, but as in all lingering grudge matches, a little humility on both sides could have probably solved it.

One morning, just before what would have been his twenty first birthday, Chatty responded to the rumor that his adversaries chased his mother into her apartment with their dog. This promoted his simmering anger to a state of rage, and he set out to destroy him. While allowing his rage to increase, he ran after them brandishing a sword.

Chatty caught up to the two culprits alone in the front stairwell, near the lobby. He yelled at the top of his voice "I am the Incredible Hulk" while stomping his feet down simultaneously. His would be victims responded by firing three rounds from a forty five caliber handgun at very close range. Dwayne never really stood a chance, but with blood gushing from these mortal wounds, he managed to climb eight flights of stairs to his mother's apartment before he died.

Often some of the war's survivors sit around and talk about the old days. The legend of Chatty always comes up though more than thirty years has passed since he died. His life epitomized unfulfilled potential, his death a tragedy. We remember his heart and character, the zany antics, and his gift of gab. I wonder what influence he may have had on today's youth if he nurtured his gifts and the war overlooked him.

Hassan

When I think of Clyde, I think of an old picture I had of him, shooting a jump shot up at Branch Brook Park. I knew his whole family, his mother and two older sisters. From the beginning, Clyde ran with the wrong crowd, Muffy, Richie and those other Junior Masons as they called themselves. He tried to be tough, or was it just mischievous… I'm not really sure any more. All I know is that I liked him as a person.

As a teenager, Clyde had to do a little time, maybe at Jamesburg or Annandale. Once he came home he just did not act the same to me. He was more like one of the fellas than a tough guy wannabe. He'd play ball, shoot the shit, smoke a little pot, but no more of the outlandish criminal type stuff, that is except for maybe his habit.

A few years before he died, his family had left Columbus and moved into Stephen Crane Village near the Newark-Belleville border. Like so many others in Newark, he became afflicted with a deadly germ. He stayed relatively close to home, and very seldom was seen around the Avenue. At the request of my father, I went to see him before his demise. We talked for a little while and I enjoyed the conversation. The next time I was at his mother's house was the day of his funeral. When I first wrote this book, I didn't know what I wanted to say about Clyde. I know now what I'd say is that I liked him, and as a person miss him.

Josh

Larry, Josh as we called him, was one of the 10 Sheffield Drive Jones Boys clan. He was neither the oldest the youngest the smartest or the strongest of them, just the closest to me in age. We also share a nephew, so I guess that makes kind of us family.

His playing football was not all that special either, because almost all of his brothers played football. One of his brothers was already coaching high school football when Larry was still in junior high. Sure he was good but not great. He had to earn his notoriety in other ways.

In our age group, Josh was one of the wilder ones, but avoided the trouble most of that group suffered. He did no real jail time and stepped around serious drug use as well. He was tough, and a good fighter, but more good natured than most other Junior Mason gang he hung out with. Though more playful than vicious, he was certainly not one to be pushed around.

I remember a few incidents involving him, mostly fights or near misses. The legend that stands out the most in my mind was the time he came to the rescue of his youngest brother, who got jumped in the parking lot between building 84 and 74. As the story goes, Josh came on the scene carrying a baseball bat and his reputation. Instead of wielding it against his brother's attackers, he offered it to them to use on him. They panicked and fled the area without a victory.

After completing high school, Josh settled down for the most part to work as a painter and raise a family. I'd see him a lot when I lived at the bottom of the hill. We would laugh and reminisce. Always more a friend than antagonist, I enjoyed his wit and his counsel. He died suddenly of a heart attack I think as a shock to all that knew him.

Kevin

My sister married Kevin's father, so I guess that kind of makes me his uncle by marriage. His family and mine lived on the same floor in the same building. I counted his two older brothers as my best friends.

Kevin always seemed to suffer from one allergy or another when he was a kid. He avoided direct physical confrontations, yet most of the guys his age in the neighborhood avoided conflicts with him. He always dressed nicely.

Kevin first started getting into trouble shortly after his natural birth mother passed, and when his father started dating again. They retained him in the same school grade about that time. He began using drugs at a young teen age, and he was caught with burglar tools. After a few minor scrapes with the juvenile justice system, he straightened himself out legally. He did however continue his drug use and had a very active sex life.

Kevin took a custodial job with the Board of Education, and maintained employment there throughout his adult life. After some years he even managed to stop using drugs. He met a young lady he liked enough and fathered a daughter with her. Just before the child's birth Kevin discovered he had caught the HIV.

Kevin tried to hide his illness from all his friends, but his brother informed me about the diagnosis shortly after Kevin told him. I never let on that I knew. It was not until about six months before he died that Kevin, deteriorating rapidly in health told me. When I told him I knew and had known for at least three years he admitted being angry, embarrassed, but relieved. Kevin slipped away quietly in the company of family a few weeks before his thirty eighth birthday.

I was honored to be a pallbearer at his funeral. I remember that in the six years before he died, Kevin visited my home more often than all my other friends and family combined. He never asked me for anything more than maybe a splash of cologne. I truly miss him.

Harold

I always worried about Harold. He was the baby of the family, and never really left home. He had some kind of problem with being alone. Some folks said he liked men sexually, but I really don't know or care to know. I'd rather prefer to stay in denial about that.

Harold was sensitive and he was also a drunk who got beat up often while in his drunken stupor. I never saw him play basketball, but he talked like he was better than the rest of us. He lied pathologically. He often made promises and did not keep them. I often heard how he tried to convince other people he was my age, and accomplished what were my deeds. I never got a straight answer from him about whether he completed high school or not. I would get very angry with him about his drunkenness, his lying, his friends, and his secrets. Like I said, he was the baby, my youngest brother, and I worried about him.

Harold possessed perhaps more good characteristics than his bad ones. He was generous to a fault, and would give his last to help someone out of a jam. He'd nurse many people outside the family who were sick or suffering. He performed favors for people so they could continue doing whatever they were doing,

and he befriended everyone. He provided a door to door income tax preparation service, often helping those friends he served find those questionable deductions and larger than average returns. Harold was musically inclined and played several woodwind instruments. He often returned to our old high school and voluntarily helped out with the band, chorus, dramatic productions, and the track team. Yeah, although he played no basketball or football, he did run... very very fast. Harold even put together a track team made up from Columbus Homes residents' children and coached them to the Penn Relays.

Harold has been dead a decade now. Some say it was an overdose. Heroin, cocaine, and alcohol were found in his system at acutely high doses at his death. Some say it was murder since the large amount of money he possessed the day he died disappeared before his arrival to the hospital. Some even said they believed he committed suicide due to grief. He had not been the same for a few months since a friend he lived with and cared for died. I prefer to believe he tried to help a friend celebrate, accidentally went overboard, and in doing so died unafraid.

Picture courtesy of Michelle Cook Bryant

Years after his death, I met the lady whose party Harold went to the night he passed away. I knew she felt tortured because of the state she was in. She also retold the story of events in her apartment the night leading to Harold's death. I told her I held no grudge about my brother's death and that relieved her somewhat, but my forgiveness alone won't purge her of the demons coming from those events.

Harold left a great many friends behind. They showed up at his wake in such large numbers and contributed financially to insure he did not end in the pauper's burial ground.

His wake was loud and boisterous. Most people said good things about him, while some spoke of the negatives anecdotally. I was angry with him for what he did to himself. I was angry with him for what he did not do for himself. Maybe I still am angry with him, but at least, I no longer worry about him.

The WICKEDS

Following the decline of a real summer recreational program out of the Columbus Homes Community Center, an increasing amount of activity took place at Branch Brook Park. Points of pride were the Columbus Homes basketball teams, first CHAD and then the WICKEDS. The name of the team adorned several buildings in the complex as spray painted graffiti.

Every one who played against them thought they knew exactly what the team name WICKEDS meant. Surely the reputation of Columbus Homes had something to do with it. The high crime rate and drug use must have contributed to the name. The team's aggressive play and argumentative style added credence to the belief their name represented pure evil. Yet whoever thought those characteristics represented the team name meaning would all be wrong for the name meant more, much more.

I stood near Building 84 looking at the name when Richard Thomas, one of the players came by. Richard was the younger brother of a good friend, so we engaged in some light-hearted banter. I pointed to the name, and told him all the negatives surrounding it, and he looked at me with the smile of the cat that just cornered the mouse.

"Well," Richard said to me, "if this was chess you have just made your last move. I've got you checkmated. The name says one thing but only on the surface. Each letter represents an attribute of our hearts and what we strive for through life." He then gave the following meaning for each letter.

> Wisdom,
> Intelligence,
> Character,
> Knowledge,
> Education,
> Determination,
> Success

Over the years I have used the same simple formula while teaching recovering addicts to improve their self-esteem. I tell them that regardless of the negativity in their lives, they can easily change by attaching positive attributes to each letter of their name. When they complete the exercise and repeat the positives as if they believe them, they tend to feel better about themselves, all because of the meaning given to me by Richard of the W.I.C.K.E.D.S.

That same young man, Richard, lost his life while in another part of the city. Someone shot him down in cold blood, just to take the white double goose down bomber jacket he wore at the time. It is a shame that someone with such high qualities should lose his life in that way, taken by someone who obviously did not know the meanings of the words.

The Wounded

Everyday, in the presence of those left wounded in some way from the battles and the casualties reminds me of the war. I wonder what caused where we lived to become a war zone. Was it the appearance and use of drugs? What part did having attitudes of superiority or superior goals play? Or was the primary cause the frustration of not being able to achieve those lofty ambitions? Were these the cause for such a level of human failure?

Sometimes the loss of a loved one by death or separation causes sufficient pain to change once noble attitudes and behaviors to despicable motives and acts. The best of us are susceptible to lose that small edge we may have if the circumstances warrant it. The best are often the ones hurt the most by their human failings when the pressures that society places on them forces them to back away from a dream or perform less than at their desired level of excellence.

These best tend to be the aggressive, the physically able and the near geniuses, who find no legal outlet within their eight by eight foot square to show their true worth. So they intrude on the space of others because it is easier than to expand their own space. They use drugs and violence, and they coerce those weaker than themselves. If they do not die, they end up incarcerated, hooked on themselves, or on death dealing drugs.

There is hope. All did not die, and all were not jailed. Some live to be shining examples to the rest of us that to give up on ourselves, and take the illegal shortcut is to lose the battle and the war. Some will change. Some will get to the point where they throw off their weaknesses and exercise their strengths. They will be the real leaders, for they will be able to show you the error of their old ways.

However, it is up to you to determine the road you will follow, whether you win this war, whether you die from it, or if you become the wounded reminders in someone else's war stories.

Rocky

Rocky Rossi lived in Building 82, I believe an only child. He made friends with pretty much the whole neighborhood whether they were Black, Puerto Rican, or of his own Italian heritage. Rocky was always that sort of character, somewhat outgoing, mild and reserved, and just plain nice. And no one can doubt he is a war survivor. In fact he has survived two of them; first he lived through jungle battles during Vietnam as a member of the U.S. Army Special Services Unit call the Green Beret, and then of Columbus Homes. It's hard to say which war wounded him the most.

For years after returning from Vietnam, Rocky could be seen walking around the neighborhood with one or more cameras strapped to himself. He used then to chronicle events and people following a free-lance lifestyle, often selling photographs to the Star Ledger or other papers if what he shot was newsworthy. He was always willing to talk photography with Curtis, Jimmy, Alex, or myself. Coming to think about it, he was willing to share that passion of his with damn near anyone who befriended this scraggly dressed, skinny white boy, who continued to hang around Columbus, long after white flight was over.

Rocky still lives and in fact I saw him just a few days ago walking up Park Avenue. Only God knows how and why he made it this long. For years he could be seen in a somewhat aimless pattern in downtown Newark. I would run into him around Military or

Washing Park while he reeked of the smell of beer. Rocky drinks and drank more than a little bit, knows that he is an alcoholic but desires not to fight it. I think surrender is so hard for such a survivor of our war and others.

Chester and Reggie

The story of Chester and Reggie speaks of what true friendship is all about, because Chester Jones and Reggie Howard were just that. Often when men are as close as these two were, some may believe there may be more to it than friendship, something vulgar, but with these two that was not the case. They were both as fiercely heterosexual as men get, and yet their bond was closer than what many pairs of lovers ever achieve.

From the time of their youth in the projects, both living up on Sheffield Drive, Chester and Reggie had their close kind of friendship that went beyond talk. They knew each other's family, hung out together, shared common interests, and planned Columbus reunions together. Even after Reggie's family moved out of Columbus to the Weequahic section, he still found his way over to hang out with Chester.

I can't think of one time in my life that I thought they were not friends. Even into adulthood, when Reggie would commute into Newark from his home in Plainfield, somehow he and Chester caught up with one another. Chester also reciprocated in seeking out Reggie. Neither one had to look too hard for the other. They always seemed to know where the other was, or where he was going to be.

Shortly before I left Newark, Chester died. His death was sudden, a heart attack maybe caused his untimely demise. It is my understanding that before anyone found out about it or was able to tell Reggie, Reggie passed away as well, the very next day, and just as suddenly as his friend.

Innocent Bystander

He was after all only an innocent bystander, walking by the bar as a fight broke out inside. He stood there for only a minute, looking and listening to the sound of excitement. He never noticed the security guard out of place at the scene, or the gun that was drawn, or the bullet that hit him in the jaw, shattering it. He was after all, only an innocent bystander.

The Woodson Tragedy

They were such nice people. Mr. and Mrs. Woodson also had very nice children, a lot of them. I remember liking two of the girls, Linda and Vickie, and playfully chased them around Frank's laundry room on Crane Street. The sons were pretty cool too. I just wish I knew how at the time to approach them when Mr. and Mrs. Woodson both died in that car crash on Rt. 22. They were friends I could not help through their pain and sorrow, friends I thought of often, and had lost seemingly forever. It's only been recently that over the Internet through e-mail have I found contact to all through one of the surviving family members.

Mrs. Jones

She was the mother of a still close friend. She and her husband were closely associated to my father as well. How her tragedy befell her no one knows for sure. Her blindness in one eye may have contributed but I'm unsure about that. Some rumors contend she jumped while under the influence of alcohol, but I refuse to believe that. I believe she accidentally lost her balance while washing windows and fell eleven fights to the ground. She lived for three days, broken inside and out. Such physical pain I hope I never need to endure. War breeds accidents too.

In the Can

Life is precious and innocent life is even more so. A newborn innocent life ended up in the can; its life snuffed out by someone who believed in the righteousness of his or her act. Was it the mother? Was it the father? Was it someone who witnessed the delivery? Who knows? The dead baby ended up in a garbage can, lying still and unnoticed for days, until the stench of the rotting body escaped. The parents never revealed themselves. Only the stench remained behind from the act.

The Rapist

One day when I was about six years old I heard a bunch of voices yelling that there was a rapist in Building 74. A large number of men from the neighborhood ran into the building and up the stairwells. Then I heard the men caught him, beat him up, and chased him out of the projects. I didn't know what a rapist was, and in all the years I lived there I never really found out. It makes me wish now that somebody had yelled "drug dealer" on the Avenue, the first time one showed up.

Carol

She has not been the same since she saw whatever she saw. She has spent most of her adolescence and adulthood in asylums and group boarding homes. The rumor has it that she witnessed a coat hanger operation of some other girl, pregnant before legalized abortion, before the catchy phrase words of "teenage pregnancy" became popularized in describing the condition, and before Planned Parenthood. And Carol has never been the same since.

Muffy

As young boys he intimidated me by challenging me to fights which we never had and starting trouble. As a teenager he became friendlier, then occasionally roughing away cigarettes, petty change, and the like. He played hooky, drank wine, and the other things the young toughs did... gang wars, petty crime and time. By the time we were in our twenties we became more comfortable around each other. In manhood as in youth his aggressive tendencies got him into trouble, however let there be no mistake about this man. He possessed great potential, both physically and intellectually. And I consider him to mean more to me than merely an acquaintance.

Muffy served time in the state penitentiary for something stupid. During the incarceration, it became necessary for him to undergo emergency surgery, as prison doctors discovered that he had a critical heart condition. Their malpractice nearly killed him and further damaged his body. Although his heart did not work right, it was not weak. He obtained a parole, sued the State, and won out against them. He completed his parole, married a very intelligent, educated, and beautiful woman, and then moved out of state. He thrived where a lesser man would have caved in to the system. He survived the old day as a victor and less a casualty of war. I have heard he passed away at his home in Ohio, but of this I am not sure.

Lois

In comic books, it took Superman to win over Lois Lane by doing what no other man could. The Lois I speak of took the same coaxing because she was a very attractive prize. The men who tried to get with her needed daring, courage, toughness, and athletic prowess and they tended to be outcasts, trouble makers, and criminals. Instead of winning her heart with a sweet song, tenderness and understanding, they took her with thrills, excitement, and drugs.

For years she wallowed in their lifestyle as a mere shadow of her former beauty. The men did not stick to her but the drugs did. The strangest part of her story involves her brother. As a self proclaimed wonder on the Newark police force, his once close relationship with his sister disintegrated with her continuing drug problems. And me, I wondered for years where his true loyalties were... and why.

Throughout the eighties and the nineties Lois struggled with the addiction lifestyle, before she discovered the superwoman she truly was herself. She managed to get herself together, and the last time I saw her, the girl was looking good again. I am told she has died since the initial writing of this book.

112

Andre F.

I don't know how he is doing now, but my once next door neighbor where he lived with his mother and great grandmother started out with great promise. We, the older young men on our floor took a hand in his basketball playing education. He went on to star at Irvington High School, then went to Texas to play college ball. He didn't last long.

Andre came back home and fell into the culture of the neighborhood, and in love with a pretty young lady. He would have done anything for her, and usually did, almost like Samson would have done for Delilah. She unintentionally ended up sapping the moral strength from Andre, as he succumbed to her charms and indiscretions.

Andre after not being able to secure the love he sought, found the love of another girl, that white girl better known as crack. Despite many attempts to kick her out of his life, this girl seduced him into a dream world, leaving him helpless, homeless, and satisfied with his style of life. One of the last times I saw him, he was telling me of his love of life on the streets of Newark, and of what he learned from it. He would always tell me that he was doing well off of drugs, but would lose jobs then fall back into drug use. The last time I saw Andre, he was working in a health care field. I haven't heard about him in years and don't know how he is doing, but I hope he has learned to love himself more that that girl.

Mikey

Mikey ran faster than just about everyone in the neighborhood. He was well known, relatively popular or at least liked and respected. He fought decently and bullied no one. If somebody stepped to him physically, more than likely he gave better than he got. He was no punk. He was one of the boys.

Mikey also excelled academically, and got away from home for a college education. College changed him, or maybe brought him out of the closet. You see Mikey was gay, and all the time we were growing up, he hid that part of himself from us. When he came

113

home from school, he stayed away from us, choosing to associate with his gay friends. We would see him from time to time, strike up brief conversations. And then, he would go his way as we went ours. It seems as if his lifestyle got in the way of our friendship.

As the years went by, increasingly Mikey was seen alone and only in passing. He'd always ask about old mutual friends, and he always seemed lonely. Then several years ago Mikey claimed to have fathered a daughter. I ran into him on the bus on day and asked how having a child fit into his lifestyle. He said fatherhood made this the happiest time of his life. I also asked him why he kept avoiding old friends over the years. He said he feared we would reject him because of some mistakes he made in his life.

I believe true friendship lasts a lifetime, and that a good friend is hard to find. The earliest days of our lives tried and tested Mikey's friendship and loyalty. We ate at each other's home, knew each other's families, fought each other, and together against all others. Yet here he was telling me we all had pushed him away. I told Mikey he was wrong about us, but I wonder really. I wondered if years of separation could change good friends into strangers we once knew. And if time can do that, what else can?

Gussie

I thought Gussie was dead. For years I saw him languishing in the strip mall that once was the Food Fair Supermarket, lying, bumming change, drinking, drunk, or high. I was sure that the lifestyle he lived would mercifully kill him as it had so many other men from the projects. Merciful would death have to be because Gussie had a rough time at life from the very beginning.

Born to an Italian descendant mother in the early 60's, Gussie was of a darker hue than his brother Joe. I am sure that distinction made him catch hell in the social environment of the Columbus Homes community. He grew up tough, just like his brother, made friends, and did what he could to belong. It seemed like the need to belong led him past the loving home of his mother and out to the streets.

114

Even after his family moved out of the projects Gussie still hung out there. And after the projects were closed and eventually blown up, Gussie still hung out in the neighborhood, his relationship with his mother, brother, and children strained, and with his addiction firmly in control.

Mercy did not happen, salvation did. Gussie was whooped by his addiction. It gave him pains the drugs could no longer cover up. He became sick... sick of his addiction, sick of what he had to do to feed it, and sick of what it did to him. So about two years ago, Gussie surrendered, gave up. He gladly allowed himself to get arrested when he had drugs in his possession. He did time in the prison drug program at Delaney Hall. Eighteen months later he came out a remarkably different person.

I saw Gussie on my last visit home and I could hardly believe my eyes. Gussie looked good physically. He spoke of his trials and tribulations working his recovery process. He said he has a sponsor and a home group, and that he is making meetings, things I tried to get him to do when I was in the field, and living across from where he used to hang. He takes commitments, is becoming known as a public speaker, and is taking care of what he must. Gussie has a renewed relationship with his brother and his 84 year old mother could not be more proud of him. And I am glad that despite what I thought may be best for him, God it seems had another plan.

Muhammad

I am so proud of this brother. Let me tell you he was one of the best ball players ever to come out of Columbus. Speed, agility, ball handling, and that sure left handed jump shot got him noticed in high school and got him a scholarship to Morgan State. After being a star everywhere he had played, he was not ready to sit on the bench at Morgan State, so he left school...before the end of the first semester.

Muhammad was lost. He wandered around his life, giving in to the whims of the neighborhood. He played summer ball in the park and hung out. Fatherhood failed to make him more responsible and the neighborhood continued to piss all over his game of life. He became a runner, crack head, and a scam artist for a while. Then it happened, a one year stint in the county jail. It may have saved his life.

I ran into this brother when he got out, determined to shed his life of the demons that had imprisoned his heart and mind. Muhammad completed treatment successfully, and has stayed clean ever since. He has moved back to the head of his family, to his wife and all her children. He works hard every day to support them, and is doing real well at everything. He has left his playing at life game behind him and is now living life.

Jimmy

As youths, we thought Jimmy could accomplish anything he wanted to. He was an above average student, and though not that big or tall, he performed athletically at a superior level to most of the neighborhood. He possessed excellent moves, a strong arm, fast feet, and a good blend of aggressiveness and intelligence. He picked up a trumpet for the first time in junior high school and

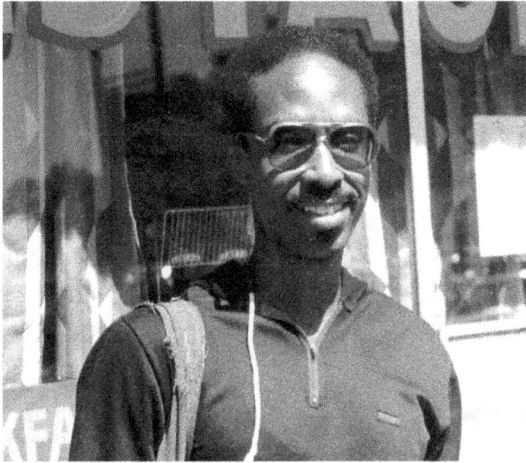

held the first seat within a year without the benefit of private lessons. He definitely had star potential.

Jimmy could have very easily fit into the same mold as the tough guys, but did not. Even the tough guys knew that messing around with him put them into a position for defeat. They backed down before he did. His fatal flaw was the belief he was better than his peers were. His snobbish arrogance led him to taunt others, and to drug use when he entered high school.

Though he finished high school, he initially failed to follow through with a college education. With the help and guidance of his father he obtained a position at the post office, but eventually lost it behind his use of drugs. His life became one of unfulfilled potential.

Then something happened. Jimmy saw his unhappiness and re-evaluated his life in retrospect. He admitted he wasted a good fifteen years and squandered away some very good opportunities. He vowed to defeat the rule of drugs over his life, and for more than two decades he has lived up to that promise he made to himself.

Since Jimmy ended his drug use he completed college with a degree majoring in computer science, and a minor in music. He regained his competency in playing trumpet, began writing music, and earned mastery in jazz. Today, he manages computer systems on Wall Street when he wants to, teaches young Black men in the area of Afro-centric studies, delights himself as a part time musician, and fights against the system as a tax revolutionary.

Jimmy fulfilled our beliefs and expectations about him. He overcame the seemingly impossible. When all of us put ourselves into living instead of escaping life and expose our best characteristics, the rest of us succeed too.

Walter and Stephen

Tenacity and intelligence accurately describe the characteristics belonging to Walter and Stephen. They owned well endowed athletic prowess at a young age and received the added blessing of strong supportive family structures. Their good hardworking parents cared greatly how their sons fared in such a tough neighborhood.

Walter and Stephen handled themselves quite capably. They defended themselves against bullies, and shirked away from no challenge. They put a strong emphasis into learning from new situations, and gained a high level of academic excellence. They each earned scholarships to a local private high school, which, if not a first for the neighborhood, then certainly a first for our group. They excelled at that academic level too, for they received the reward of acceptance by and eventually graduation from Ivy League universities.

I spoke to Walter since I originally wrote this story. He accomplished a lot for himself. After graduating from the University of Pennsylvania and the Wharton School, he purchased a home for his parents. He worked for awhile with one of the big oil companies in Texas that paid him quite handsomely for his effort. He became the controller for the quasi-public statewide transportation agency, and assisted in some capacity with the finances for the City. He now has his own CPA firm. When I asked when he expected to make his first million, he only laughed in response. He married a lovely young lady, made himself independent of employers, and remains very happy with his life.

All things considered, Stephen's luck pales in comparison to Walter's. He only managed to graduate from Columbia University with a degree in Architecture. He failed to escape from the employment by Black owned and major architectural firms in the New York City vicinity. At last contact, he commutes between Harlem and Philadelphia weekly to work a second "job" designing and building sets for a Black theatre troupe there. He drives an economy car. He rented an apartment along with his wife and children. He may earn in the high five figures (but quite possibly I may have tremendously underbid his income). I can only hope my luck equaled his.

Omar S.

There once was a wild kind of boy who lived in Columbus, very, very good with his hands, and with a penchant for hanging around older boys. He was not intimidated by them and held his own with them and with their exploits. His mother, he had told me had a problem with the juice, his father a relative unknown. And he as one of the oldest boys of his family, had to maintain a tough reputation, something he did, initially to his regret, and eventually to his salvation.

While nearly the age of manhood, this boy took part of a murderous action with two older guys. To make matters worse, the manner in which their victim was disposed made news in two

119

states. They were all eventually caught, tried, convicted, and sent up the river for a very long time. Our boy grew into manhood in New Jersey's top maximum security prisons, Trenton and Rahway.

Initially he took the tact that many from the hood had taken, changed his name and made a conversion. I am unsure on whether or not that his conversion was half hearted, but he told me that what came with it was a jailhouse hardened toughness that may have kept him safe, but did not move him where he needed to be.

After some years in stir, one of his crime partners was released to pursue a professional life of boxing. Around the same time, our man who had strengthened his body with weights, began to take advantage of the educational opportunities then afforded by the prison to strengthen his mind. He also began to wonder why so many of those who gained their freedom from the correctional institution always seemed to find their way back. High school equivalency became the lead in to higher education focusing on the plight of the incarcerated. After a final change in his spirit, and twenty years in the slam, he emerged dedicated to helping released convicts from returning to jail.

He now lives up to his name Omar, meaning flourishing and speaker depending on whether you acknowledge the Arabic or Hebrew meanings. He is flourishing as he speaks to and for ex-convicts as the head of an ex-offender program sponsored by American Friends Service Committee.

George

George resented being alone as a child. He responded to conflicts by crying, and feared fighting when he was challenged. Once he got into a fight, however, refusing to battle back brought on the threat of a confrontation with his father. Since his father terrified him, he fought and lost many encounters. He let teasing bother him, and his bad temper thrust him into situations he failed to escape without a struggle. Negotiations always fell through in this neighborhood. So win or lose he fought back or ran away.

George enjoyed growing up and had fun but felt unhappy more times than he actually let on. He lacked self confidence and displayed difficulty holding conversations, so he read a lot. Because he despised his self imposed isolation he sought for ways to gain acceptance from others. He ended up alone, ridiculed, angry, or accommodating. The other guys he tried associating with left him out of team games or made him one of the last guys picked to play. Even when chosen, they ignored his presence on the field of play and just froze him out of the game. He lacked hustle and coordination early on. George hated being last, and believed for many years the other guys just hated him instead of believing they played better than he did.

George possessed some good points but his faults prevented him from getting ahead. He was smart and a decent student, but he played the class clown part to gain attention and threw temper tantrums. He learned to play a few musical instruments but practiced irregularly and his musically inclined talents decayed. He worked hard to make some money as a youth, kept employed, but managed his earnings poorly. He envisioned a positive future, but lacked direction to get there.

He faced a troubling adolescence after his father left home. Shyness, embarrassment, and anger prevented him from discussing his thoughts and feelings with his friends and family. He drank alcohol and smoked cigarettes to show off or fit in. Some people he tried to impress said they liked him better without the rum and coke he sneaked into high school classes. He stopped drinking in a dependent manner, and graduated high school.

He enlisted in the Navy during the Vietnam Conflict, just hoping to get away from home. There he began writing descriptive letters and poetry as an outlet to his imagination. He matured physically and gained more confidence in his athleticism. Many of his old faults also surfaced as temper tantrums and led to disciplinary actions, changing his fast promotions to a bust. Somehow he managed an honorable discharge after his 42 month enlistment ended.

George returned to the projects and entered the local community college. He participated in many campus activities and graduated magna cum laude. He continued his education at a major university in the desert Southwest that preferred its Black male students to be athletes. He joined an elite Black fraternity dedicated to community service as his campus activism continued. He completed a course of study, graduated from the university, and returned home.

The neighborhood had changed. Different people lived there and the place felt uncomfortable to him. George moved to another part of the city where he became involved romantically with a lady he met during his years at the community college. He lacked the experience at maintaining personal relationships and this intimate involvement failed horribly. He moved back to the Southwest six months after his love life collapsed, searching for his identity.

Four years after leaving Newark, George returned because his mother was dying, and remained there for nearly two decades. He began working out many of the internal conflicts that caused him to act out and show off. He improved his anger responses somewhat, and became relatively comfortable with his life. He still needs improvement with team play. He did marry for a short time to the same woman he had failed with before. Some things just never change.

George may never fulfill his potential but then again maybe he will. He survived the wars and battles from Columbus Homes and serves on the front lines. For most of the last two decades, he worked as an addiction counselor, teacher, or social services worker, all of which are sort of like a medic. He pulled the wounded off the battlefields all over Newark and Phoenix, stitched them up, before sending them back out there to survive or die by their effort or the lack of it.

I am that George.

Survivors

Mrs. Ernestine Davis
Mr. Eddie Davis Sr.
Mrs. Ethel Hines
Mr. Lonnie Jones
Mrs. Reynolds
Ms. Rufus
Mrs. Elsie Stephenson
Mrs. Augusta Workfield
Ms. Jean Irving
Miss Janey
Mrs. Hicks
Carol Cook
Glenn Cook
Michael Cook
Michelle Cook
Phyllis Cook
Janet Andrews
Tommy Andrews
James Bracey
Sheila Bracey
Anthony Baskerville
Venus Baskerville
Bernard Brooks
Frances Brooks
James Brooks
Lois Brooks
"Jun" Brooks
Said Brooks
Yusef Brooks
Kaye Brooks
Michelle Brown
Walter Brown
Gerald Buglione
Rocco Buglione
David Burks
Jimmy Burks

Kim Burks
Stacy Burks
Gussie Caporella
Joe Caporella
Curtis Clark
Sam Clark
Vincent Cobb
Laverne Coleman
Linda Coleman
Lonnie Coleman
Richard "Peanut" Coleman
Kevin M. Dailey
Ralph Dailey
Toni Dailey
Yvette Dailey
Douglas Darby
Melvin David
"Bubbles" Echols
Michael Echols
Todd Echols
Steven Echols
Darlene Echols
Vickie Echols
Lizzie Echols
Al Edwards
Crystal Edwards
Jeffrey Edwards
John Elmore
Barbara Jean Epps
Christine Epps
Linda Epps
Jerry Fisher
Andre Frazier
Barbara Frazier
Kamela Gettis
Fred Gettis

Wesley Gettis
Allan Green
Cynthia Harrison
Ellen Harrison
Bob Henwood
Richard Henwood
Alfonso Hicks
Gloria Hicks
Gwendolyn Hicks
Theresa Hicks
Susie Howard
Jackie Howard
Maureen Howard
Robin Howard
Jeffrey Howard
Angie Irving
Anthony Irving
Countess Irving
John Irving
Tracy Irving
Linda Irving
Richard Irving
Trudi Scheland Iwanus
Anita Jackson
Carey Jackson
Joyce Jackson
Michael James
Adele Jenkins
Annabelle Jenkins
Jessie Jenkins
"Pinky" Jenkins
Rosie Jenkins
Deniece Cunningham Jones
Denise Jones
Donald Basir Jones
Jerome Jones
Lonnie Jones
Margie Jones
Marvin Jones
Michelle Jones

Ronald Jones
Vernon Jones
Hamed Kidd
Ruthie Kidd
Clarence Poochie King
Gail King
Margie King
Shirley King
Cynthia Mann
Ronald Mann
Anitra Martin
Marie Martino
Eddie McDaniels
Jackie McCrae
Richard Mcrae
Brian Melvin
"Jun" Minatee
Paulette Minatee
Sheila Minatee
Glenn Wheeler Muhammad
Bernard Roach M. Muhammed
Helen Norris
Hubert Norris
Dorothy Palumbo
Juanita Pendergrass
Sam Pendergrass
Abdullah "Poochie" Plant
Dennis Tariq Rasheed
Gwen Reynolds
Gina Reynolds
Hilton Reynolds
Pam Reynolds
Ronald Reynolds
William Reynolds
Valerie Reynolds
Ethel Sawyer
Alfred Scott
Carol Scott
Gabril Scott
Glenn Scott

David Scott
Henry Scott
Iona Scott
Lacy Scott
Omar Shabazz
Barbara Smith
Jimmy Smith
Larry Smith
Leroy Smith
Monroe Smith
Carol Spiers
Joan Spiers
Paul Spiers
Lanell Stephenson
Richard Stephenson
Rodney Stephenson
Yolanda Strange
Cheryl Strange
Stanley Thomas
Barbara Triplett
Benjamin Triplett
Betty Triplett
Charles Triplett
Elaine Triplett
Darlene Vining
Dean Vining
Dorene Vining
Reginald Vining
Allan Walker
Bernadette Walker
Cranston Walker

Dorian Walker
James Walker
Madora Walker
Stephen Walker
Greg Ward
Missy Ward
Patty White
Eddie Najee Wilcher
Herbert Wilcher
Tyran Wilcher
Ann Willis
Bud Willis
Gail Willis
Harry Willis
Michael Willis
Linda Woodson
Victoria Woodson
Albert Timmy Workfield
Augusta Workfield
Carl Skippy Workfield
Cathy Workfield
Dorothy Workfield
Lillian Worfield
Muhammad H. Workfield
Ricky Workfield
Roxanne Plant Workfield
James E. Wynn
Jordan T. Wynn, Jr.
Gilda Zaragoza
Jose Zaragoza

plus many more and their families

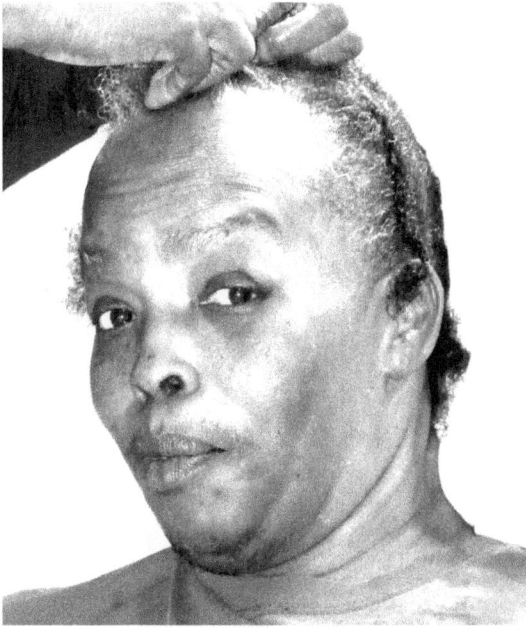

Picture courtesy of James E. Wynn

Picture courtesy of James E. Wynn

Picture Courtesy of James E. Wynn

Picture courtesy of James E. Wynn

Picture courtesy of James E. Wynn

Picture courtesy of James E. Wynn

Picture courtesy of James E. Wynn

Picture courtesy of James E. Wynn

Picture courtesy of James E. Wynn

My best friends of more than 50 years from left to right are
Jordan Wynn, my brother Michael, and James Wynn

Honorable Mention

Mrs. Lucy Mae Cook
Mr. George H. Cook
Mrs. Mary Wynn
Mr. Jordan T. Winn Sr.
Ms. Virginia Howard
Mrs. Julia Epps
Mr. Lynwood Bracey
Mrs. Mary Bracey
Mrs. Jane Dixon
Mrs. Luann Fisher
Mrs. Harrison
Mrs. Vi Herbin
Mr. William Herbin
Mrs. Doris Plant
Mr. Bill Price
Mrs. Catherine Sawyer
Mr. Jerry Sawyer
Ms. Chi Chi Strange
Mrs. Bethune (Granny)
Mr. Clark
Mrs. Clark
Mrs. Dickinson
Ms. Harrison
Mrs. Jackson
Mrs. Letha Jenkins
Mr. Horace Jenkins
Mrs. Beatrice McCrae
Mr. Richard McCrae
Mrs. McDaniels
Mr. Robinson
Mr. Scott
Mrs. Scott
Mr. Taylor
Mrs. Walker
Mr. Judge Walker
Mrs. Woodson
Mr. Woodson
Mr. Harold Workfield

Mr. Wesley
Father Nativo
Casey Andrews
"Woosy" Andrews
Mr. Wilcher
Mrs. Wilcher
Norman Beale
Anthony Bracey
Melvin Bracey
Timothy Bracey
Dennis Brooks
Clyde Hassan Brown
Teddy Brown
Daryl Burks
Ethel Burks
Robert Butler
Walter Ali Cabel
Don Carroll
Simone Clark
Pete Coleman
Robert Keith Coleman
Harold Cook
Leonard Cunningham
Beatrice Daily
Lois Darby
Celestine Davis
Diane Davis
Eddie Davis Jr.
Pat Davis
Queen Esther Davis
Russell Davis
Raouf Dixon
Antonio Duran
Michael Early
Charles Echols
Elaine Echols
David Eng
Jerome Fisher

Jay Foster
Brenda Frazier
Ernestine Frazier
Timothy Frazier
Terry Fuller
"Bug-eyed" Freddie
Sonny Gettis
Valerie Gettis
Joseph Greer
Alfred Harris
John Harrison
David Da'oul Harrison
Floyd Hayman
Sherwood Hayman
Willie Herbin
Larry Hight
Gary Hinton
Pat Hinton
Peggy Hinton
Darrell Da'oul Hines
Dwayne Hines
Bernard Howard
Butch Howard
Gregory Howard
Reginald Howard
Diane Howell
Clifford Hughes
Dee Dee Hughes
Chuckie Hughes
Sonny Jackson
Charles "Foots" Jenkins
Gordon Jenkins
Horace Jenkins
Sarah Jenkins
Tommy Jenkins
Chester Jones
Dennis Jones
Leroy Jones
Marshall Jones
Margie Jones

Johnny Kearny
Tommy Kearny
Anthony King
Gregory McCray
Ronnie McCray
James Ricky Miller
Herbert Norris
Efrain Padilla
Milton Padilla
Abdur Reynolds
Pete Reynolds
Bonnie Rogers
Brenda Rogers
Charles Rogers
Evelyn Rogers
Sheila Rogers
Jerry Sawyer
Sharon Sawyer
Butch Scott
Deniece Scott
Louis Scott
Charles Singleton
Richard "Dickie" Smith
Wannie "Tank" Smith
Adrian Soler
Derrick Strange
Stephen Strange
Ronald Turner
Eric Vining
Lorenzo Vining
John Vining
Altrathea Ward
Ernest Ward
Jackie Ward
Pam Ward
Sheila Ward
Thornell Ward
Cody Wilcher
Ronnell Wilcher
Logan Wilkerson

Bruce Wilson	Norman Workfield
Julie Workfield	Tariq Wright
Marshall Workfield	Kevin Michael Wynn

And so many more

Picture courtesy of James E. Wynn

Add your own memories of those mentioned or not mentioned.

_____

_____

_____

_____

_____

_____

_____

_____

_____

_____

_____

_____

_____

_____

_____

_____

_____

_____

_____

_____

_____

_____

147